Crafts Magazine

make it **MeRRy**

A Medley of Christmas Crafts

Copyright © 1999
Creative Publishing international, Inc.
5900 Green Oak Drive
Minnetonka, Minnesota 55343
1-800-328-3895
All rights reserved
Printed in U.S.A.

President: Iain Macfarlane
Director, Creative Development: Lisa Rosenthal
Executive Managing Editor: Elaine Perry

Make It Merry created by: The Editors of Creative
Publishing international, Inc. in cooperation with Crafts
Magazine – PRIMEDIA Special Interest Publications.

Project Manager: Linnéa Christensen
Art Directors: Brenda Lindhorst, Stephanie Michaud
Project Editor: Deborah Howe
Copy Editor: Janice Cauley
Illustrator: Earl R. Slack
Desktop Publishing Specialist: Laurie Kristensen
Print Production Manager: Patt Sizer

Vice President, General Manager: Harry Sailer
Publisher: Susan Wilmink
Editor: Miriam Olson
Senior Editor: Kim Shimkus
Associate Editors: Miriam Hughbanks, Sherrill Kolvek
Assistant Editors: Amy Koepke, Carol Martino, Doris Roland
Administrative Assistant: Diane Littlejohn
Art Director: Dena L. Jenkins
Designers: Lucy Blunier, Barb Spink

Printed on American paper by: World Color Press
10 9 8 7 6 5 4 3 2 1

Creative Publishing international, Inc. offers a variety of how-to books. For
information write:
    Creative Publishing international, Inc.
      Subscriber Books
    5900 Green Oak Drive
    Minnetonka, MN 55343

Library of Congress Cataloging-in-Publication Data
Make it merry : a medley of Christmas crafts.
    p. cm.
    ISBN 0-86573-175-6 (hardcover). -- ISBN 0-86573-176-4 (softcover)
    1. Christmas decorations. 2. Handicraft. I. Creative Publishing
International.
TT900.C4M285 1999
745.594'12--dc21   99-23412

make it MERRY

A Medley of Christmas Crafts

CREATIVE
PUBLISHING
international

MINNETONKA, MINNESOTA

Contents

the great outdoors

techniques

HeaveN
ON
earth

With the bright light of a great star, heavenly angels heralded Jesus' birth. Remember the true meaning of the season with symbols of light, love, and song.

QuiLt
aNGeL

aLtHOUGH HeR BODY AND WINGS are made
from wood, it is the cHeRISHeD scRAp from your
GRANDmOtHeR's QuiLt that makes this ANGeL so
speciaL. sHe HAS SUCH a sUNNY DIspOSITION AND
woNDeRfuLLY weatHeReD Look that
you wiLL waNt to DIspLAY HeR
yeAR-ROUND.

Materials

- ¼" x 8" (6 mm x 20.5 cm) pine wood, 2 ft. (0.63 m)
- Wood: 1½" (3.8 cm) wood ball knob, 1" (2.5 cm) wood heart
- Acrylic paints: tapioca, peach, black, rose
- Brown antiquing medium
- Clear spray varnish
- Paintbrushes: 1" (2.5 cm) flat, 10/0 liner
- 5" x 7" (12.5 x 18 cm) used quilt piece
- Dried florals: Spanish moss, German statice, seven ⅜" (1 cm) dried red rosebuds
- 1 yd. (0.95 m) ivory satin ribbon, ⅛" (3 mm) wide
- 12" (30.5 cm) white wired paper twist
- Small picture hanger
- Scroll saw
- Pattern Sheet
- Miscellaneous items: tracing and graphite paper, pencil, scissors, fine sandpaper, tack cloth, paper towels, white craft glue, hot glue gun, water-soluble pen

1 *Patterns & Cutting:* Trace the half patterns onto tracing paper, following the instructions on the pattern to make a complete pattern for the wings, body front and body back. Place the patterns on wood and trace around them; use the scroll saw to cut out. Use graphite paper to transfer the dashed lines on the body front pattern to the body front, and cut out with the saw.

2 *Body Assembly:* Sand the cut edges smooth; remove sanding dust with tack cloth. Place body front on quilt scrap, and trace around the inner edge with water-soluble pen, as shown in the Step 2 illustration. Cut out the quilt. Place the body front on the body back and glue together with craft glue. Let dry.

3 *Basecoating:* Refer to the Painting Instructions and Techniques on page 160. Let paints and finishes dry between colors and coats. Use the flat brush and rose to paint the body front/back and arms, tapioca to paint wings and heart, and peach to paint the wood knob for the head. Sand painted pieces for an antique look, sanding heavier on the edges.

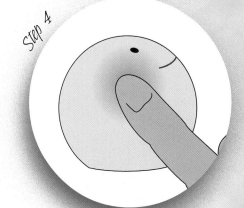

4 *Face:* Place knob flat side down; flat side will be back of head. Use the liner brush and refer to the photo to paint a rose mouth. Dot black eyes above the mouth. See the Step 4 illustration to blush cheeks with rose using a finger.

5 *Antiquing:* Follow the manufacturer's instructions to use the flat brush and antique all wood surfaces. Wipe excess with paper towels. Spray wood with 2 coats of varnish, following manufacturer's instructions.

6 *Assembly:* Glue the quilt scrap to the body back inside the body front edges. Refer to the pattern to glue top of wings behind neck, and arms to upper body front, matching the shoulders; see the Step 6 illustration. Glue head to body. Let dry. Attach hanger to upper back of wings.

7 *Hair & Halo:* Hot-glue Spanish moss to head for hair. Bend paper twist into a circle for halo; twist ends together. Slip halo onto head and hot-glue at back. Cut six 6" (15 cm) ribbon lengths and tie into bows. Randomly hot-glue 5 rosebuds, 3 bows and statice to halo front. Hot-glue statice to hands and heart on top of statice. Hot-glue a rosebud and bow to each side of heart.

Cathedral window
ornaments

These fabric ornaments are an adaptation of the classic cathedral window quilt pattern. Traditionally done in cottons and calicoes, jewel-tone silks really glow like stained glass.

Materials

FOR EACH ORNAMENT

- Two 6½" (16.3 cm) squares gold Doupioni silk or taffeta
- 2" (5 cm) squares: 2 each of jewel-tone fabrics, such as red velvet or aqua silk, and 1 of fusible knit interfacing
- Scrap of polyester fiberfill
- 12 gold seed beads
- 10" (25.5 cm) gold cord for hanging loop
- Miscellaneous items: ruler, scissors, rotary cutter and mat (optional), straight pins, sewing machine and matching gold thread, iron, sewing needle

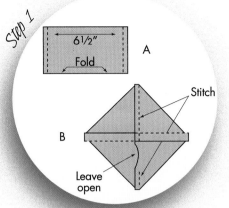

Step 1

6½"

Fold

A

B

Stitch

Leave open

1 *Stitching:* See the Step 1A illustration to fold each gold square in half. Pin on both short ends, stitch ¼" (6 mm) seams, and press the seams open. Match the seams together along the open edges, and pin. Stitch ¼" (6 mm) seam, as shown in the Step 1B illustration, leaving an opening for turning. Finger-press the seam open.

2 *Folding:* Turn the squares right side out, and slipstitch the openings shut. Press lightly; you should now have 2 double-layered fabric squares that look like the Step 2A illustration. Fold the square as shown in 2B, so the corners just meet in the center. Pin the corners in place, and tack them together. You should now have 2 pieces that look like the folded paper game you played when a child, with numbers on the outside and messages on the inside.

3 *Joining:* Place the squares side by side, as shown in the Step 3A illustration, and hand-stitch them together along 1 side. Fold the squares back-to-back; see Step 3B. Hand-stitch together along the opposite side, so the squares form a tube.

4 *Forming Window:* Refold the tube so the seams are matching, as shown in the Step 4A illustration. The diamond shape in the center will become the cathedral window for the contrasting square of fabric. Measure the diamond-shape window along its sides; it should be approximately 2" (5 cm).

5 *Stained Glass:* Fuse the interfacing square to the back of the contrasting stained glass fabric square. Trim the square to be slightly smaller than the window, if necessary. For a 2" (5 cm) window, the square should measure 1⅞" (4.7 cm). Center the stained glass fabric square within the window shape, and pin in place.

6 *Rolling:* Roll the folded edges of the window around the raw edges of the stained glass fabric. Pin in place, and secure the folded edge by blindstitching it to the stained glass fabric. See the Step 4B illustration and the photo, and stitch 1 side at a time.

7 *Stuffing:* Hand-stitch 1 of the open ends closed. Lightly stuff some fiberfill inside. Knot the hanging cord into a loop; stuff the knotted end into the remaining open end of the ornament. Pin loop in place at 1 corner, and tack. Stitch the remaining side shut, catching in the hanger at the corner. Stitch 3 gold seed beads at the center of each side of the ornament, where marked by X's in the Step 4B illustration.

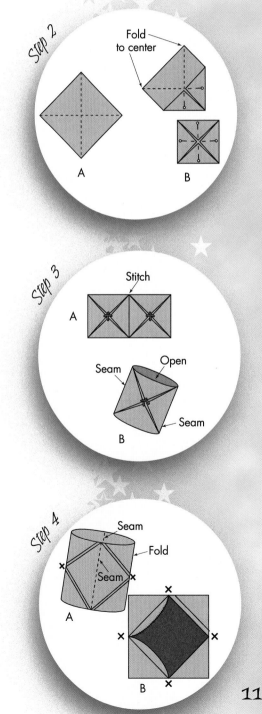

Step 2

Fold to center

A

B

Step 3

Stitch

A

Seam

Open

Seam

B

Step 4

Seam

Fold

Seam

A

B

11

Light up the Night
vest

tURN ON THE GLITZ AND GLAMOUR with an appliquéd lamé string of lights on a black felt vest.

Materials

- Adult-size black felt vest
- ⅛ yd. (0.15 m) each, 45" (115 cm) fabrics: lamé: turquoise, magenta, gold; marble print satin
- ½ yd. (0.5 m) paper-backed fusible web
- 5 yd. (4.6 m) metallic gold flat braid trim, ¼" (6 mm) wide
- Kreinik metallic braids: Medium No. 16 gold 002HL and Very Fine No. 4 metallic gold 002HL, black 005
- Miscellaneous items: pencil, tracing paper, straight pins, scissors, embroidery needle, iron, fabric glue, sewing machine and matching thread (optional)

1 *Patterns:* Trace the patterns onto tracing paper along the solid and dotted lines, and cut out. Dotted lines represent where bulb overlaps socket. Follow the manufacturer's instructions to apply the fusible web to the wrong side of the fabrics. Trace the number indicated on the patterns onto the paper backing of the appropriate fused fabrics, and cut out the appliqués. Refer to the Embroidery Stitches on page 158 for couching, blanket and running stitches.

2 *Fusing Bulbs:* Refer to the photos and the Step 2 illustration to lay out the 22 light bulbs on the vest fronts and back, or create your own layout. Pin bulbs and sockets in place. Follow the manufacturer's instructions to fuse the sockets, then the bulbs. Fuse the plug to the lower left vest front.

3 *Light Cord:* Begin at the plug on the lower left vest front to lay out the cord. Loop and turn the braid, and continue up the left vest front, around the back of the neck and down the right vest front. Pin the braid as you go, as seen in the Step 3 illustration. Be sure not to get it too close to the vest edge where the gold flat braid will go. Couch the Medium No. 16 gold braid to the vest using the Very Fine No. 4 gold braid.

4 *Embroidering Bulbs:* Use Very Fine No. 4 gold braid to work blanket stitches around each bulb; see the Step 4 illustration. Use Very Fine No. 4 black braid to work running stitches ⅛" (3 mm) inside the edges of the plug and sockets.

5 *Finishing:* Glue or machine-stitch the flat gold braid trim around the vest edges and armholes.

Step 2

Step 3

Step 4

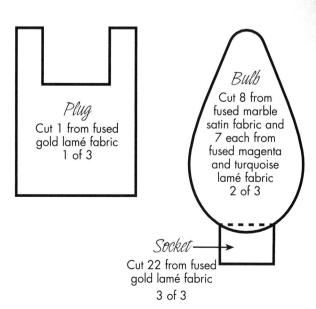

Plug
Cut 1 from fused
gold lamé fabric
1 of 3

Bulb
Cut 8 from
fused marble
satin fabric and
7 each from
fused magenta
and turquoise
lamé fabric
2 of 3

Socket —
Cut 22 from fused
gold lamé fabric
3 of 3

CLay pot
nativity

Share the true meaning of christmas with your children; this charming nativity is one that kids can actually handle. cleverly crafted from small clay pots and wooden balls, this project is a perfect family holiday activity.

Materials

- Wooden shapes: *balls:* one each ³⁄₄" (2 cm), 1" (2.5 cm), 1¹⁄₂" (3.8 cm); six 1¹⁄₄" (3.2 cm); *flowerpots:* one each 1" (2.5 cm), 1¹⁄₂" (3.8 cm); ¹⁄₁₆" *(1.5 mm) thick:* 10 medium teardrops; 7 small teardrops; 8 small ovals; 3 squares; ¹⁄₈" *(3 mm) thick:* one each 1¹⁄₂" (3.8 cm) circle, 3³⁄₄" (9.5 cm) star

- Acrylic paints: blush, black, white, mauve, blue, sage

- Paintbrushes: Nos. 4 and 8 flat; No. 1 liner; ¹⁄₄" (6 mm) stencil

- Clay pots: eleven 1⁵⁄₈" (4 cm); one 6" x 11" (15 x 28 cm)

- Spray clear acrylic sealer

- Doll hair: white wool, dark brown yarn, auburn curly

- ¹⁄₈" (3 mm) wide satin ribbons: 18" (46 cm) each burgundy, white

- Six ³⁄₈" (1 cm) flat white buttons

- Natural raffia

- 18" (46 cm) jute twine

- Cotton fabrics: 5¹⁄₂" (14 cm) square white, 7" (18 cm) square burgundy/cream/green plaid

- 6" (15 cm) of 18-gauge wire

- Textured snow paint

- Natural excelsior

- Miscellaneous items: paint palette, paper towels, toothpicks, fine-line black permanent-ink marker, thick white craft glue, ruler, scissors, craft stick

1   *Painting:* Refer to page 160 Painting Instructions and Techniques. Let dry between paint coats and colors. Two coats of paint may be needed with some colors. Use the No. 4 flat brush to basecoat the 1" (2.5 cm) and six 1¼" (3.2 cm) balls with blush. See the Step 1 illustration to paint the details. Use the stencil brush and mauve to dry-brush the cheeks. Dot the 2 eyes with black; use a toothpick and white to highlight. Draw eyebrows with black marker.

2   *Painting Clay Pot Bodies:* See the Step 2 illustration to paint the inside and top rim of 3 pots and 1 entire pot with mauve. Paint the inside and top rim of 1 pot and 1 entire pot with blue. Paint a 1" (2.5 cm) mauve strip down 1 pot; paint the remainder with sage. Paint a 1" (2.5 cm) white strip down 1 pot; paint the remainder with blue. Reverse colors for another pot. Paint 1 entire pot with white. Use the black marker to draw a wavy line around the bottom edges and to outline the 1" (2.5 cm) strips.

3   *Wise Men:* Stack pots upside down and glue as follows: mauve pot on top of blue-rimmed pot, blue pot on top of a mauve-rimmed pot, and sage/mauve pot on top of a mauve-rimmed pot. Glue a 1¼" (3.2 cm) painted ball on top of a pot, centering the face on the mauve strip.

4   *Wise Men Arms:* See the Step 4A illustration to paint ³⁄₈" (1 cm) of the round ends of 6 medium teardrops with blush for hands. Paint the rest of the teardrops in pairs: blue, mauve and sage. Use the black marker to draw a stitching line around each sleeve and cuff. Match the arms to top pot; glue arm tops to pots. Angle arms toward the center, and center them around face. Refer to the photo to paint the 3 squares for gifts; decorate with the black marker. Glue the squares to the hands. Spray with acrylic sealer.

5   *Wise Men Hair & Beards:* Apply glue to the head and chin areas; press on varying lengths of white hair. Leave 1 wise man bald on top; trim hair as desired. Cut three 4¼" (10.8 cm) lengths of ribbon; glue around each head. Glue a button to hair or headband. Tie small ribbon bows, and glue to the gifts.

6   *Baby Jesus:* Refer to the photo and the Step 6A illustration to crisscross and glue 3" (7.5 cm) lengths of raffia to 1 side of the wooden circle for the manger. Glue the 1" (2.5 cm) painted head into the 1½" (3.8 cm) wooden pot; paint pot and back half of head with white. Use the black marker to draw stitching lines as shown in the photo and the 6B illustration. Spray with acrylic sealer. Tie a bow from 4" (10 cm) of jute; glue to the center front of the pot rim. Glue a button to the bow. Glue the baby onto the raffia faceup.

(Continued)

15

7 *Mary and Joseph:* Stack and glue the blue/white pot on top of a mauve-rimmed pot for Joseph; Mary is the single white/blue pot. Glue head balls on top of pot bodies, centering faces over strips.

8 *Mary & Joseph's Arms:* See the Step 4B illustration to paint ¼" (6 mm) of the rounded end of 4 small teardrops with blush. Paint the rest of the teardrops in pairs: blue and white. Paint 4 small ovals, 2 white and 2 blue. Draw black stitching lines around the edges of the white teardrops and ovals. Match arm colors to the pots, and glue the ovals near the top of the pot for the upper arms. Refer to the photo to glue the pointed end of the teardrops on top of the oval for the lower arms. Spray with acrylic sealer.

9 *Finishing Mary & Joseph:* Refer to Step 5 to glue dark brown yarn for hair and beard. Fold the white fabric square in half diagonally; drape the folded edge across Mary's head for headdress; see the Step 9 illustration. Tuck and glue the ends inside the pot. Tie a bow from 5" (12.5 cm) of the white ribbon; glue to Mary's neck. Glue a white button beneath the bow.

10 *Shepherd:* Glue head to upside down white pot. Follow Step 8 to paint and glue white arms. Spray with acrylic sealer. Refer to Step 5 to glue curly auburn hair. Tie a bow from 4" (10 cm) of jute and glue to the center neck. Follow Step 9 to make a plaid headdress. Tie 4½" (11.5 cm) of jute around the headdress and head. Refer to the photo to form the wire into a staff and glue to the hands.

11 *Lamb:* Glue the 1½" (3.8 cm) ball inside a small clay pot for the body, and the ¾" (2 cm) ball inside the 1" (2.5 cm) wooden pot for the head. Refer to the photo to glue the head to the side of the body near the bottom. Paint 4 medium teardrops for legs, 1 small teardrop for tail, 2 small ovals for ears and the outside and bottom of the head pot with black. Lay the body pot on its side; refer to the Step 11 illustration to glue on the legs. Use a craft stick to dab the snow paint onto the body, covering the tops of the legs and fringing the head. Place the tail and the ears on the body; the snow paint will act as glue.

12 *Lamb Face:* Dot a white eye on each side of the head; highlight with black. Use the liner brush to paint a white nose and mouth line on each side of the head. Spray with acrylic sealer. Cut 6" (15 cm) of ribbon; tie around the lamb's neck into a bow.

13 *Finishing:* Use the black marker to outline the star with a wavy line accented with dots. Prop the 6" x 11" (15 x 28 cm) clay pot on its side on a flat surface. Glue the star to raffia, and then raffia to the pot top, slightly off center. Place excelsior in the pot and arrange figures as desired.

Luminaries date back to the days when shepherds lit fires at night to guard their flocks. Let your Light shine outside this season on your stairs, sidewalk or deck.

Nativity Luminaries

Materials

- Five 8½" x 14" (21.8 x 35.5 cm) brown paper bags
- Tung oil
- No. 2 flat paintbrush
- 10 votive candles
- Pattern Sheet
- Miscellaneous items: tracing and graphite paper, pencil, sand

1. *Pattern:* Trace the patterns to tracing paper. Place each pattern on a bag, with the design 2" (5 cm) from the bottom. Slip a piece of graphite paper between the bag and the pattern, and use the pencil or stylus to lightly transfer the pattern to the bag.

2. *Painting:* Use the paintbrush to paint the patterns with several coats of tung oil to achieve a transparent effect; see the Step 2 illustration. Use several thin coats, rather than 1 thick coat, because an overloaded brush may cause the oil to bleed out of the pattern area and ruin the design.

3. *Finishing:* When bags are dry, fill each with 2" (5 cm) of sand, and place votive candles in the sand. Use 2 candles per bag to increase the transparency. Never leave lit candles unattended. These luminaries are designed for outside use only.

Step 2

stitched
Seasonal sentiments

Cards from the store are fine for most people, but your closest friends and family will appreciate the extra effort you put into handmade greetings. Cross-stitched on perforated paper, these season's greetings are a cinch even for beginners.

Materials

- 5" x 7" (12.5 x 18 cm) perforated paper: silver, antique brown, white
- 1 skein each 6-strand embroidery floss in colors listed in Color Key
- No. 24 tapestry needle
- 5½" x 9" (14 x 23 cm) card stock: red, blue, light green

- Pattern Page 167
- Miscellaneous items: spray adhesive, scissors

Ornament Stitch Chart
Color Key

SYMBOL	DMC #	COLOR
X	415	Pearl Gray
o	676	Lt. Old Gold
I	680	Dk. Old Gold
=	729	Med. Old Gold
I	813	Lt. Blue
◆	824	Vy. Dk. Blue
N	826	Med. Blue
—	310	Backstitches
★	310	Bow Placement

1 *Preparation:* Refer to the Perforated Paper/Plastic General Instructions and Stitches on page 159 and the Stitch Charts here and on page 167 to cross-stitch each design using 2 strands of floss. Use 1 strand of Black No. 310 floss to backstitch. Each square on the Chart represents 1 square of perforated paper. Symbols correspond to the colors in the **Color Key**.

2 *Stitching:* Stitch the designs on the following perforated paper colors: Rejoice on silver, the Ornament on antique brown and the Bear on white. Refer to the Stitch Chart to thread an 8" (20.5 cm) length of 6-strand black floss through the border above the ornament design. Tie floss in a bow; trim ends.

3 *Card Assembly:* Fold card stock in half to 4½" x 5½" (11.5 x 14 cm). Trim perforated paper to ¼" (6 mm) (3 rows) from stitched border. Lightly spray back of stitched design with adhesive. Center Rejoice and Bear on card front with fold at top; center Ornament with fold at left.

mesh star tree topper

This delicate star made of wire mesh is simply made by folding 2 pieces and joining them together at the edges. Hung atop your tree by a delicate cord in the back, it will proclaim the message of the birth to all.

Materials

- 12" x 16" (30.5 x 40.5 cm) silver wire mesh, 1/8" (3 mm) pattern*
- 2 yd. (1.85 m) silver trim, 5/16" (7.5 mm) wide
- Quick-drying fabric adhesive
- 6" (15 cm) fine silver cord or wire for hanging loop
- Pattern Sheet
- Miscellaneous items: tracing paper, pencil, scissors, craft knife, straight pins, ruler, round toothpicks, sewing needle

*(See Sources on pg. 176 for purchasing information.)

1   *Pattern:* Trace the star pattern, including folding lines, to tracing paper, and cut out. Place pattern on the mesh, and pin. Use the scissors to cut around the pattern; leave pattern pinned to the mesh.

2   *Folding Note:* Handle the wire mesh gently, and when folding use a ruler to get straight edges. However, the creases should not be knife sharp, but soft and rounded, as seen in the photo. If creases are too sharp, the wire mesh will be difficult to work with and get out of shape. Use a craft knife to help pry apart folded pieces and the joining edges, if necessary, by poking the thin blade end in and lifting up gently.

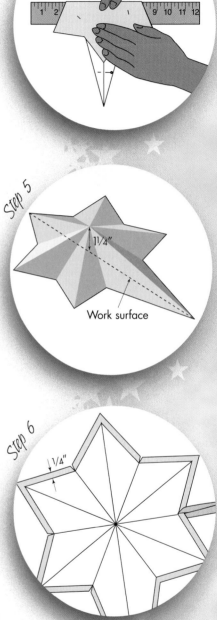

Step 3

3   *Folding Lines 1-3:* Refer to the pattern to fold lines 1-3 in numerical order. Begin by folding the top half of the star, as seen in the Step 3 illustration. Place the ruler along Folding Line 1 and make a straight, gentle crease. Fold so the pattern is folded in on itself for all 3 folding lines. After each fold, gently bend the star back to its original open position.

4   *Folding Lines 4-6:* Repeat Step 3 to fold the mesh along Folding Lines 4-6 in numerical order, except fold the mesh the other way, so the wire mesh folds in on itself and the pattern is on the outside.

Step 5

1¹⁄₄"

Work surface

5   *Center Point:* After the 6 folding lines have been made, return the star to its open position. Reshape the center point gently. Unpin and remove the star pattern. The center point should be about 1¼" (3.2 cm) high, when the edges rest on a flat work surface; see the Step 5 illustration.

6   *Second Star Half:* Pin the star pattern to the remaining wire mesh. Use the scissors to cut around the pattern; **adding ¼" (6 mm) around all edges.** Clip the ¼" (6 mm) edge to the pattern at the 6 short pattern points; see the Step 6 illustration. Leave the pattern pinned to the mesh.

Step 6

¼"

7   *Joining Edge:* Place the ruler along 1 edge of the pattern, and fold the edge up and over it. Continue to make soft folds all around the star, 12 in all. This will make a joining edge, to hold the star pieces together.

8   *Folding Second Star Half:* Repeat Steps 3-5 to fold and shape the star, while maintaining the joining edge folds. Gently fold up the joining edge, off the paper pattern. Remove the paper pattern, and place the 2 star halves together, with center points facing outward. Put the smaller star inside the larger star, so the smaller star cut edges meet the larger star joining edge foldlines. Gently refold the joining edges down, to hold the star halves together.

9   *Trim:* Glue trim along the edges of both star halves; use a toothpick to spread the glue and apply in hard-to-reach areas. Use a needle to insert the fine cord or wire, 2½" (6.5 cm) up from the end of the long point. Tie a knot, and trim the ends, leaving a 3" (7.5 cm) loop for hanging.

Double Blessings pillows

This darling angel pillow is cute-as-can-be whether rendered in fused fabric appliqués or hand-colored with crayons. The real blessing is that each method is equally simple.

Materials

FOR EACH PILLOW

- 45" (115 cm) cotton fabrics:
  1/3 yd. (0.32 m) green print,
  8" x 13" (20.5 x 33 cm) tan solid,
  4" (10 cm) square yellow print;
  for the appliquéd pillow only: 2"
  (5 cm) square each pink solid and
  red print, 3" (7.5 cm) square
  yellow print, 3" x 5" (7.5 x
  12.5 cm) white print, 2" x 4"
  (5 x 10 cm) each brown print
  and green stripe, 5" (12.5 cm)
  square green print

- 10" x 15" (25.5 x 38 cm)
  cotton batting
- Polyester fiberfill
- Four 1/2" (1.3 cm) red flat buttons

FOR THE APPLIQUÉD PILLOW

- 1/4 yd. (0.25 m) fusible web

FOR THE HAND-COLORED PILLOW

- Binney & Smith, Inc.
  Crayola® crayons: tickle me pink,
  macaroni-n-cheese, brown, red, black,
  goldenrod, red orange, green, white

- Pattern Sheet

- Miscellaneous
  items: iron, tracing paper, pencil,
  scissors, 8" x 13" (20.5 x 33 cm)
  freezer paper, masking tape, fine-line
  black permanent-ink marker, air-
  soluble marker, cotton swab,
  powdered blush, ruler, straight pins,
  sewing needle, sewing machine and
  matching threads, paper towels

Hand-Colored Pillow

1 *Preparation:* Repeat Steps 1 and 2 from the Appliquéd Pillow, except in Step 2 only trace the Pillow Front/Appliqué Guide, and use the black marker to trace the angel and heart only. Do not trace any dotted lines yet. Use a very light touch and work with a circular scribbling motion. Lightly color the face and hands tickle me pink; repeat with macaroni-n-cheese. Use brown for the hair, goldenrod for the halo and star, green for the dress and red orange for the heart. Do not color the wings.

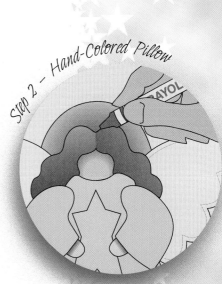

2 *Shading:* Shade the face and the hands with brown. See the Step 2 illustration to shade the halo behind the hair and the star under the hands with macaroni-n-cheese, then darken with a little brown. Shade the hair part, the dress around the star, and the back sleeve edges with black. Blush the cheeks and shade the heart outer edges with red. Use the marker to draw the stitching lines and dot the eyes.

3 *Heat-Setting:* Place the colored fabric right side up on the ironing board and cover with a paper towel. Press with a hot, dry iron, being careful not to move the paper towel. Color the wings with white. Do not press; the white disappears when ironed.

4 *Finishing:* Tape the pattern and pillow front fabric to the lightbox/window. Use the black marker and draw the hair details, eyes and penstitching lines around the halo, wings, sleeve cuff, star, neckline, hem and lettering. Follow Steps 4-5 from the Appliquéd Pillow to assemble.

Appliquéd Pillow

1 *Preparation:* Lay the tan fabric on the freezer paper, shiny side up; iron to the freezer paper using a hot, dry iron. From the green print fabric, cut 2 each border strips 2" x 12" (5 x 30.5 cm) and two 2" x 7" (5 x 18 cm) and one 10" x 15" (25.5 x 38 cm) pillow back. From the gold fabric, cut four 2" (5 cm) squares.

2 *Patterns:* Trace all 10 patterns to tracing paper with a pencil, and cut out. Tape the Pillow Front pattern to a light table or sunny window. Center the tan fabric/freezer paper over the pattern and tape. Trace the angel and heart with air-soluble marker and lettering with the black marker; see the Step 2 illustration.

3 *Fusing:* Follow the manufacturer's instructions to apply fusible web to the wrong side of the appliqué fabrics. Trace patterns as indicated onto the paper backing, leaving 1/4" (6 mm) between. Cut out and remove the paper backing. Fuse the appliqués on the tan fabric within the markings in the following order: halo, wings, dress, face, hair, star, hands, sleeves, heart. Use the black pen to add stitching lines on the wings, halo, star, sleeves, hands, lower face and heart. Dot the angel's eyes; use a cotton swab to apply blush on the cheeks.

4 *Borders:* Peel off the freezer paper; trim the fabric to 7" x 12" (8 x 30.5 cm), keeping the design centered. Stitch all fabrics right sides together using 1/4" (6 mm) seams. Press seams toward the darker fabric; do not iron the design. Stitch the 12" (30.5 cm) strips to the pillow front top and bottom. Stitch a corner square to each end of the 7" (18 cm) strips. See the Step 4 illustration to match the seams, and stitch the strips to the sides.

5 *Quilting & Assembly:* Pin the pillow front, right side up, on the batting. Hand-quilt 1/8" (3 mm) around the angel and heart and inside the border. Sew a red button in the center of each corner. Stitch the pillow front to the pillow back, leaving a 5" (12.5 cm) opening for turning. Clip the corners, and turn. Stuff with fiberfill; slipstitch the opening closed.

ebony & ivory
ornaments

Materials

- 5" (12.5 cm) square of 28-count white evenweave fabric for each ornament
- 1 skein each 6-strand embroidery floss in colors listed in the Color Keys
- No. 24 tapestry needle
- ⅛ yd. (0.32 m) satin ribbon for hanger for each ornament, 4 mm silk or ⅛" (3 mm) wide
- Polyester fiberfill
- Pattern Page 165
- Miscellaneous items: pencil, scissors, ruler, iron, sewing needle, white thread, straight pins, sewing machine

Strike a CHORD in the hearts of music lovers with this ornament trio featuring a piano's slender black and white keys. music is a magical part of the holidays with bing crosby crooning, carolers singing, and choirs rejoicing, and these would be a harmonious accompaniment to any gift with rhythm!

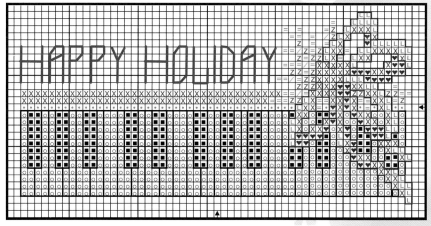

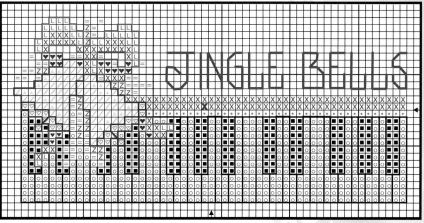

1 *Preparation:* Refer to Cross-Stitch General Instructions and Stitches on page 162 and the Stitch Charts here and on page 165 to cross-stitch the design with 2 strands of floss. Each square on the Chart represents 2 threads of evenweave fabric. Symbols correspond to colors in the Color Keys.

2 *Stitching:* Cut evenweave fabric in half lengthwise to make two 2½" x 5" (6.5 x 12.5 cm) rectangles. Stitch the design centered on 1 of the fabric rectangles; the other will be the ornament back. Work backstitches using 2 strands of floss for the lettering, and 1 strand for all remaining backstitches in the colors listed in the Color Keys and shown on the Stitch Charts. For the personalized ornament, use the Alphabet Stitch Chart to backstitch the name centered between bows. Note that there are thick and thin versions of the letters C, L, O and S to squeeze or stretch a name to better fit the space.

3 *Finishing:* Follow the Step 6 instructions on page 162 to launder, if necessary, and press stitched pieces. Cut a 5" (12.5 cm) ribbon for hanger; center and pin ends 2" (5 cm) apart to wrong side of stitched front. Place stitched front facedown on unstitched back. Stitch around edges in a ¼" (6 mm) seam. Leave a 1" (2.5 cm) opening at bottom; trim excess fabric and turn. Lightly stuff ornament, then slipstitch opening shut. With remaining ribbon, tie a bow around center of hanger.

Ebony & Ivory Color Key

SYMBOL	DMC #	COLOR
o		White
■	310	Black
·	318	Lt. Steel Gray
X	321	Christmas Red
♥	498	Dk. Christmas Red
♡	783	Med. Topaz
Z	909	Vy. Dk. Emerald Green
=	911	Med. Emerald Green
L	3801	Lt. Christmas Red
/	3820	Dk. Straw
▲	3822	Lt. Straw
BACKSTITCHES		
—	310	Black, Piano Keys
—	781	Vy. Dk. Topaz, Bells
—	815	Med. Garnet, Red Bows
—	909	Vy. Dk. Emerald Green, Lettering

Wooden dowel candles

"Light up" a set of country candles, guaranteed not to be a fire hazard. the "flames" are cleverly painted brazil nuts, and the "wax drips" are lines of hot glue.

Materials

FOR BOTH PROJECTS

- 32" (81.5 cm) wooden dowel, ³/4" (2 cm) diameter
- 7 wooden stars, 1¼" (3.2 cm) thick
- 2½" x 11½" (6.5 x 29.3 cm) wood, 1" (2.5 cm) thick
- 4 Brazil nuts
- Acrylic paints: yellow ochre, green, red, cadmium yellow

- No. 8 flat paintbrush
- Antiquing glaze
- 62" (157.5 cm) of 20-gauge wire
- Four 2" (5 cm) Phillips-head screws
- Tools: Phillips screwdriver, band saw, drill with ¹/16" bit, router (optional)
- Miscellaneous items: ruler, sandpaper, tack cloth, hot glue gun, paint palette, wire cutters, needlenose pliers

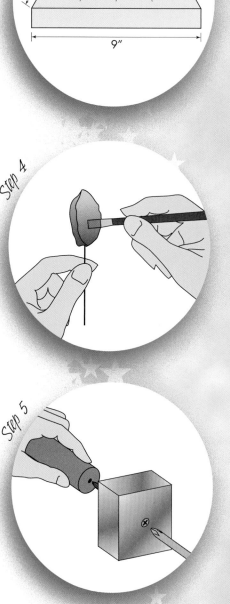

1 *Cutting:* From 1" (2.5 cm) wood, cut one 2½" (6.5 cm) square base and one 2½" x 9" (6.5 x 23 cm) base. If desired, rout the top edges. From the wooden dowel, cut the following pieces: two 6½" (16.3 cm); 1 each: 8" (20.5 cm) and 9½" (24.3 cm).

2 *Drilling:* Drill a hole into the center of each end of dowels. Drill a small hole into the large end of each nut. Mark the center of the square base, and drill through. Mark the rectangle base as shown in the Step 2 illustration, and drill through the 3 holes. Drill a hole, side to side, through 3 stars (see the green candle stars) and a hole through 4 stars from front to back.

3 *Painting Wood:* Sand all wooden pieces smooth and remove dust with a tack cloth. To make "wax" drips, apply lines of hot glue to 1 end of each dowel. Paint the bases and stars with yellow ochre. Let dry between each color and coat. Paint one 6½" (16.3 cm) dowel green and the remaining dowels red.

4 *Painting Nut Flames:* Cut four 4" (10 cm) wires. Glue and insert a wire into drilled hole of each nut. See the Step 4 illustration and begin at the top and paint with cadmium yellow, gradually blending in yellow ochre, then red at the base. Follow manufacturer's instructions to antique all painted pieces.

5 *Single Candle:* Insert a screw into the bottom of the square base, and screw up and into the green candle bottom, as shown in the Step 5 illustration. Cut an 18" (46 cm) wire, thread 3 stars drilled side to side, curling the wire around a pencil. Drill 2 holes, near the top and the bottom of the candle. Wrap the wire around the candle, gluing the ends into the holes. Cut 1 nut flame wire to ½" (1.3 cm); glue and insert onto the candle top.

6 *Candle Trio:* Refer to Step 5 to screw candles to the base. Cut a 4" (10 cm) wire; curl 1 end on a pencil. Thread on 1 star, then trim to ½" (1.3 cm). Drill a hole in the top of the center candle; glue the wire into the hole. Cut two 12" (30.5 cm) wires. Thread 1 star onto 1 wire, and 2 stars onto the other. Curl the wires; wrap around the center candle, shape as desired. Refer to Step 5 to attach nut flames.

Birch bark heart
ornament

For a nature lover's tree, this birch bark ornament done up in quantities is just the thing. it also shows true love given as a gift or used as a decoration on a present.

Materials

- Two 4½" (11.5 cm) squares of white birch bark—found on the ground outdoors, peeled off of cut firewood, or available at floral and craft stores
- Cotton ball or fiberfill scrap
- Natural color heavy-duty thread, such as button or carpet thread

- Dried florals: greens, 2 small pinecones, berry sprig
- Thick white craft glue
- Miscellaneous items: tracing paper, pencil, scissors, 3 to 4 paper clips, ruler, large embroidery or chenille sewing needle, thimble

1 *Pattern:* Trace the heart pattern to tracing paper, and cut out. Place pattern on birch bark squares and trace twice around it with a pencil. Use scissors to cut out the birch bark.

2 *Peeling:* If bark is too thick to cut, peel away a layer from the back, leaving the white on a thinner layer. Use the peeled layers for natural-colored or painted ornaments.

3 *Stuffing:* Place the 2 hearts right side, or white side, out. Put a cotton ball or scrap of fiberfill between the 2 hearts for a bit of shape. Hold the pieces together with paper clips.

4 *Stitching Preparation:* Cut a piece of thread 18" (46 cm) long, and tie a knot at 1 end. Thread through the large needle and insert the needle up through the top layer, beginning between the heart layers at the top center point; see the Step 4 illustration. Use a thimble while stitching, if desired, to help push needle through birch bark.

5 *Stitching:* Refer to the Embroidery Stitches on page 158 for how to do the overcast stitch. Stitch around the hearts with overcast stitches about 1/4" (6 mm) apart and 1/4" (6 mm) in from the edge. When you run out of thread, knot and hide it between the heart layers. If the bark is too heavy to be punctured with an embroidery needle, mark the holes ahead of time. Place the birch bark hearts on a scrap of wood, and pound needle holes through at the marked points with a small nail and hammer.

6 *Hanging Loop:* Cut the second piece of thread 24" (61 cm) long and begin stitching in the same way as in Step 4, except begin where the thread ran out. Stitch all the way around back up to the top, and knot the thread, but do not trim. Make a hanging loop about 4" (10 cm) long, as shown in the Step 6 illustration, and then go back to the center point and knot and run the thread between the layers. Trim the thread.

7 *Decorating:* Refer to the photo to glue the greens to the center top of the heart with the ends pointing outward. Glue the 2 pinecones and the berry sprig on top of the greens, centered.

Heart
Trace 2 to birch bark
1 of 1

Step 4

Step 6

4"

and they
CaLLeð him Jesus

On that holy night two thousand years ago, a baby was born and they called him Jesus. His royal birth is depicted by the bright star in the sky and his resplendent purple bunting. Stitch this timeless cross-stitch to hang in your home for years to come.

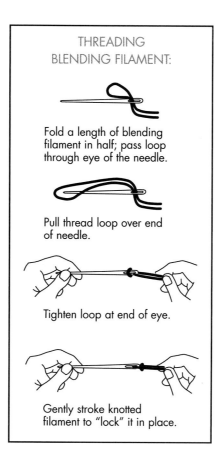

Fold a length of blending filament in half; pass loop through eye of the needle.

Pull thread loop over end of needle.

Tighten loop at end of eye.

Gently stroke knotted filament to "lock" it in place.

Materials

- 11" x 13" (28 x 33 cm) 18-count antique white Aida cloth
- 1 skein each 6-strand embroidery floss in colors listed in the Color Key
- Kreinik metallic braid: purple (012HL), hi-lustre vatican (102HL), gold (002HL); purple (012C) 2-ply metallic cord and purple (012HL) blending filament
- No. 24 tapestry needle
- Scissors
- Pattern Pages 170-171

1 *Preparation:* Refer to the General Cross-Stitch Instructions and Stitches on page 162 and the Stitch Chart on pages 170-171 to cross-stitch the design using 2 strands of floss. Each square on the Chart represents 1 square of Aida cloth. Symbols correspond to the colors in the Color Key.

2 *Backstitching:* Use 2 strands of floss to backstitch the outline of baby Jesus and his ear with No. 945 Med. Pink Beige and the eyelash with No. 801 Dk. Coffee Brown. Use purple 2-ply metallic cord to backstitch the cloth. Backstitch the lettering with 2 strands of purple blending filament and 1 strand of No. 550 Vy. Dk. Violet floss. See the illustration above for how to thread blending filament and floss on the needle.

3 *Finishing:* When stitching is complete, follow the Step 6 instructions on page 162 to launder, if necessary, and press. Mat and frame finished piece as desired.

celestial Sweatshirts

You can decorate these sweatshirts faster than a falling star. The angel's whimsical powder puff face is all smiles over her newly painted halo, and gleaming ribbon and eyelet lace stack these yo-yos up quickly.

Materials

FOR BOTH PROJECTS
- Red sweatshirt
- Fabric glue

FOR DOILY ANGEL
- White doilies: 12" (30.5 cm) Battenberg heart, 10" (25.5 cm) cluny-edge heart, 4" (10 cm) square cutwork
- 9" (23 cm) square paper-back fusible web
- 2" (5 cm) cosmetic powder puff
- 1 pair 8 mm wiggle eyes
- 1 yd. (0.95 m) each satin ribbons: 1/8" (3 mm) green, 3/16" (4.5 mm) red picot
- Dimensional fabric paints: gold glitter, yellow pearl, pink

FOR YO-YO TREE
- Sixteen 10 mm gold jingle bells
- 3 yd. (2.75 m) red/green scalloped ruffled lace, 1 1/4" (3.2 cm) wide
- Ribbons: 1/3 yd. (0.32 m) gold lamé wire-edge, 2" (5 cm) wide; 1 1/8 yd. (1.05 m) white/gold metallic, 1/2" (1.3 cm) wide; 1/2 yd. (0.5 m) red/gold metallic wired, 1/2" (1.3 cm) wide
- 2" x 4" (5 x 10 cm) fusible interfacing
- Miscellaneous items: straight pins, T-shirt board, tape measure, wax paper, craft stick, scissors, iron, fine-line black permanent-ink marker, pencil with eraser, small safety pin, wire cutters, sewing needle and matching threads, sewing machine, craft or beading wire

Preparation: Wash and dry shirt following manufacturer's instructions; do not use fabric softener. Fold shirt in half, matching shoulder seams. Mark neckline center with a straight pin.

Doily Angel

1 *Wings:* Place T-shirt board in shirt. Center Battenberg heart on shirt front 1½" (3.8 cm) below neck ribbing. Fold heart in half lengthwise and slide wax paper between layers. Lightly spread glue with craft stick onto wrong side of doily half, as shown in the Step 1 illustration. Fold down and adhere to shirt; repeat to glue remaining half using clean wax paper sheet.

2 *Gown & Collar:* Cut fusible web to fit fabric center of cluny-edge heart doily; fuse to wrong side. Refer to the photo to place heart doily upside down on shirt. Fuse to shirt, then glue lace edges. Cut a 4" (10 cm) fusible web square; cut in half diagonally. Fuse a web triangle to wrong side of one 4" (10 cm) doily corner. Remove paper backing and fuse doily together in a triangle. Fuse remaining web triangle to back, and with long edge at top, fuse collar as shown in photo, overlapping gown.

3 *Face:* Glue powder puff centered above collar. Glue wiggle eyes close together to upper face. Draw smile with the black marker. Squeeze pink paint onto wax paper. Dip eraser end of pencil in paint to dot cheeks at each end of smile. Squeeze dimensional paint yellow curls around top of head, and a gold glitter halo 1" (2.5 cm) above head, as shown in the Step 3 illustration. Match ribbons and tie a small bow at center. Pin bow to shirt below angel chin with safety pin inside shirt. Remove bow before washing.

Yo-Yo Tree

1 *Star Yo-Yo:* Cut 7" (18 cm) of gold ribbon. Tightly gather wire edges; twist ends together to form circle, and trim. Glue raw ribbon edges, then flatten to form yo-yo. Pin treetop yo-yo 1½" (3.8 cm) below top of neck.

2 *Lace Yo-Yos:* Cut 6" (15 cm) of lace and 3" (7.5 cm) of wire. Bend a ¼" (6 mm) loop at 1 wire end; insert loop through lace binding. Gather lace tightly on wire; twist ends together to form circle, and trim. Glue raw ends together. Repeat to make 15 yo-yos. See the Step 2 illustration to pin lace yo-yos 2¼" (6 cm) apart in 5 rows. Measure each yo-yo from its center; tack to shirt.

3 *Pot & Garland:* Cut 4" (10 cm) of gold ribbon. Fuse interfacing to wrong side of ribbon and refer to the photo to cut tree pot shape. Cut two 4½" (11.5 cm) lengths of red/gold ribbon. Stitch ribbons to pot, crisscrossing in the center. Stitch pot below tree using red thread. Tie a small red/gold ribbon bow, and tack to pot center. Refer to the photo and begin at top to tack white/gold ribbon to random yo-yo centers, letting ribbon curl between tacked points. Tack a bell to center of each yo-yo. Glue top of each yo-yo to shirt and pin until dry. Wait 1 week to launder shirt.

33

frosted votives

turn simple glass votive cups into beautiful frosted candleholders, with designs inspired by the lovely music heard at christmastime.

Materials

- Three 3" (7.5 cm) clear glass votive candle cups
- Three 3" (7.5 cm) squares self-adhesive vinyl
- Delta Air-Dry Perm Enamel™ Surface Conditioner
- Delta Air-Dry Perm Enamel™ White Frost
- ½" (1.3 cm) paintbrush
- Makeup sponge wedge
- Miscellaneous items: tracing paper, pencil, small craft scissors or craft knife, masking tape, straight pin

34

1 *Cleaning:* Wash the votive candle cups with warm, soapy water to remove any dust, dirt or grease. Remove any sticker residue, using nail polish remover, if necessary. Rinse and dry thoroughly.

2 *Pattern:* Trace the 3 patterns to tracing paper. Tape the designs to a light table or sunny window. Tape a square of self-adhesive vinyl over each design; trace the design with a pencil. Remove the tape, self-adhesive vinyl designs and patterns from the light table or window.

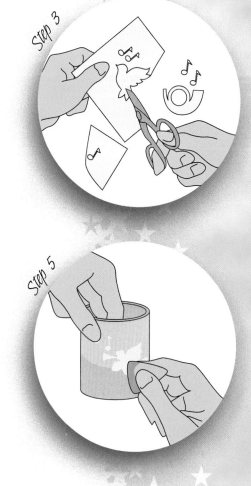

Step 3

3 *Designs:* Use small craft scissors or a craft knife to cut out the design from the self-adhesive vinyl, as shown in the Step 3 illustration. Remove the paper backing from the self-adhesive vinyl. Adhere the design to the front of each votive candle cup. Gently, but firmly, run your finger or a dull pencil around the design edges, to ensure that the paints do not leak under them.

4 *Conditioning:* Follow the manufacturer's instructions to use the ½" (1.3 cm) paintbrush to apply 1 coat of the surface conditioner to the entire outside surface of the votive candle cups. Do not paint the base, or the inside surface. Paint right over the adhered designs.

Step 5

5 *Frosting:* Follow the manufacturer's instructions to apply the white frost to the entire outside surface of the votive candle cups. Stir, do not shake, the white frost. Use a makeup sponge wedge to apply the frost as shown in the Step 5 illustration. Let dry thoroughly between coats; apply 3 coats.

6 *Finishing:* When completely dry, remove the adhered designs by using the tip of a straight pin to catch the corner of a design. This prevents scraping off the white frost. Let dry for 10 days before washing. If you choose to create your own frosting designs, keep the designs simple, with little fine-line detail.

Angel
Trace 1
2 of 3

Bird
Trace 1
1 of 3

Horn
Trace 1
3 of 3

straight ~ from the heart

these ornaments for the christmas tree are quick to make, yet full of love. combine dish towel fabric and doilies for a unique battenberg ornament, and trim wooden hearts with homespun fabric for a country look.

Materials

FOR BATTENBERG HEART ORNAMENT

- Fabric and Battenberg doilies*:
  4" (10 cm) burgundy square,
  4" (10 cm) white elongated heart,
  5" (12.5 cm) hunter green 3-leaf holly cluster
- Coordinating woven plaid dish towel fabric*, 4" (10 cm) square
- Bonded batting, 3" (7.5 cm) square
- Three 1/2" to 3/4" (1.3 to 2 cm) coordinating buttons
- Ecru embroidery floss
- Miscellaneous items: scissors, ruler, straight pins, sewing needle, white craft glue

(See Sources on pg. 176 for purchasing information.)

Materials

FOR WOODEN HEART ORNAMENT

- Two 1 1/2" (3.8 cm) wood hearts, 1/2" (1.3 cm) thick
- 12" (30.5 cm) jute
- Homespun fabric, small pieces
- Dark green acrylic paint
- Antiquing glaze
- Drill with 1/16" bit
- 2 small buttons
- Miscellaneous items: scissors, ruler, paintbrush, fine sandpaper, white craft glue

Battenberg Heart Ornament

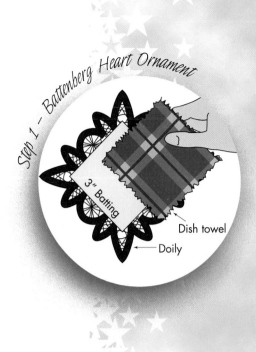

3" Batting

Dish towel

Doily

1 *Preparation:* Tear a 3¼" (8.2 cm) square from the dish towel fabric. Cut apart the Battenberg holly leaves. Refer to the photo and the Step 1 illustration to layer the burgundy square doily, the batting square and the 3¼" (8.2 cm) dish towel square; pin in place.

2 *Embroidery:* Refer to Embroidery Stitches on page 158 for how to do the running stitch. Use 6 strands of embroidery floss to sew running stitches along the edges of the dish towel square through all 3 layers of fabric.

3 *Finishing:* Refer to the photo to glue the heart doily, 1 holly leaf and the 3 buttons to the top of the fabric square. Thread a 6" (15 cm) length of embroidery floss through the top of the ornament for a hanger, and knot the floss ends.

Wooden Heart Ornament

1 *Hanging Loops:* Dip both ends of the jute cord in white craft glue; twist to compress them. Drill a hole in the top edge of each heart. See the Step 1 illustration to push jute cord ends into the drill holes. If they will not fit, drill the holes a little wider. Squirt a little craft glue in the holes; insert the cord ends. Let dry; tie the loop in an overhand knot 1" (2.5 cm) from the loop top.

2 *Hearts:* Use a wood heart as a pattern to cut 2 hearts from fabric. Trim ⅛" (3 mm) from fabric edge. Cut two ¼" x 2" (6 mm x 5 cm) fabric strips. Paint hearts dark green; let dry. Sand edges; remove dust with tack cloth. Follow antiquing glaze manufacturer's instructions to wipe hearts with antiquing glaze. Let dry.

3 *Finishing:* Use craft glue to glue fabric hearts to center of wood hearts. Knot a strip around jute at each heart top. Glue buttons over knots.

GListeNiNG staR
stocking

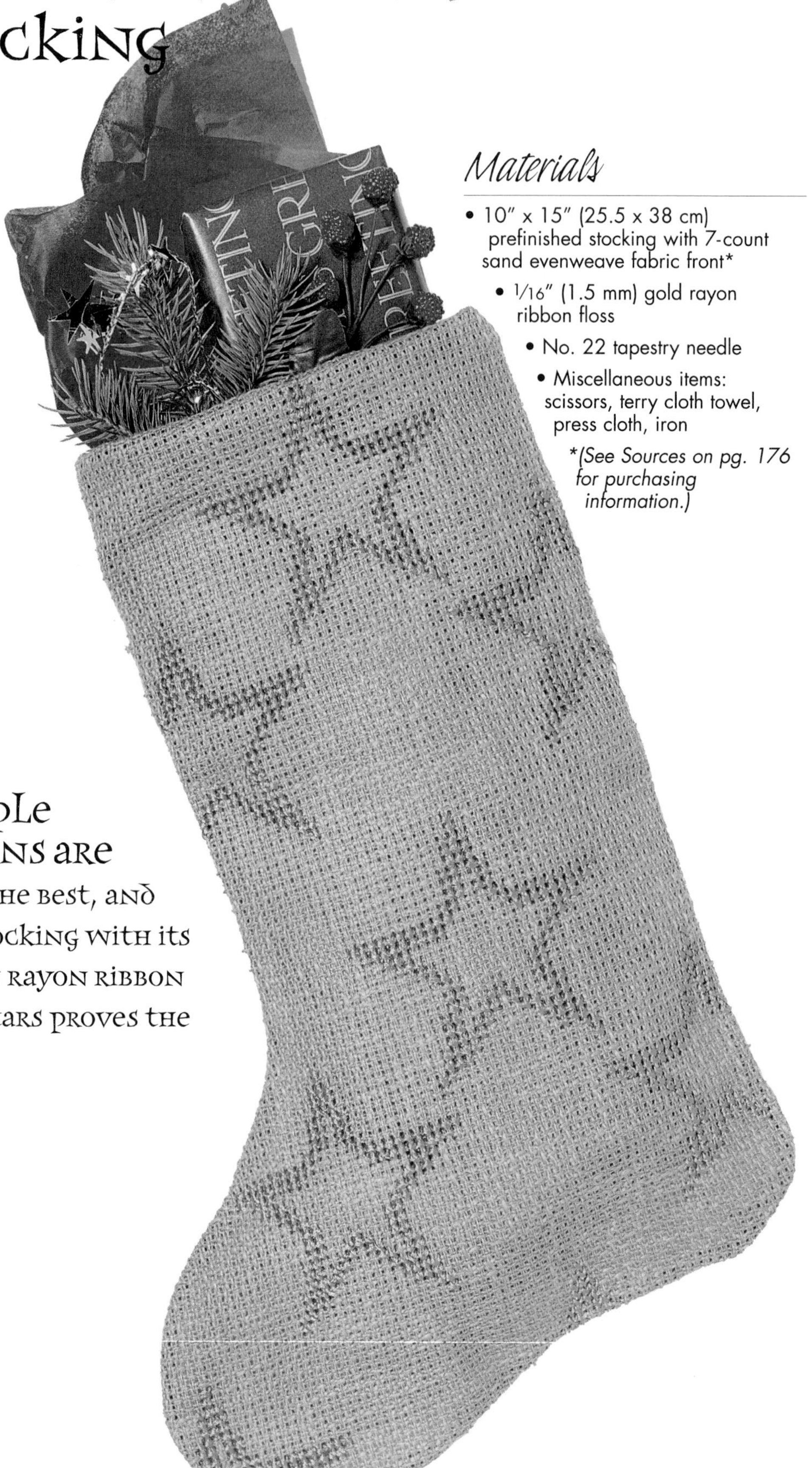

Materials

- 10" x 15" (25.5 x 38 cm) prefinished stocking with 7-count sand evenweave fabric front*

- 1/16" (1.5 mm) gold rayon ribbon floss

- No. 22 tapestry needle

- Miscellaneous items: scissors, terry cloth towel, press cloth, iron

   *(See Sources on pg. 176 for purchasing information.)

Simple
designs are
often the best, and
this stocking with its
golden rayon ribbon
floss stars proves the
point.

1 *Stitching:* Refer to the Cross-Stitch Instructions and Stitches on page 162 and the Stitch Chart. Each square on the chart represents 1 square of evenweave fabric. Count to find the horizontal center at the top of the evenweave stocking front and mark with a temporary stitch. Begin stitching the center top star 1 square down. Cross-stitch the design with 1 strand of ribbon floss; be sure the ribbon floss lies flat and does not twist.

2 *Stocking Assembly:* If you wish to make your own stocking, purchase 12" x 18" (30.5 x 46 cm) of any 7-count evenweave fabric and a cotton fabric for the back. Use the pattern to pin-mark the stocking outline centered on the evenweave fabric. Cross-stitch the star design. Mark ½" (1.3 cm) all around the stocking, except the top edge, where you should mark 1" (2.5 cm). Cut on the marked line, and zigzag-stitch twice around to prevent edges from fraying. Lay stocking reversed on backing fabric, trace around, and cut out. Pin stocking pieces right sides together, and stitch ½" (1.3 cm) seam around; leave top open. Turn top edge to the inside 1" (2.5 cm), and hem. Turn right side out; press gently.

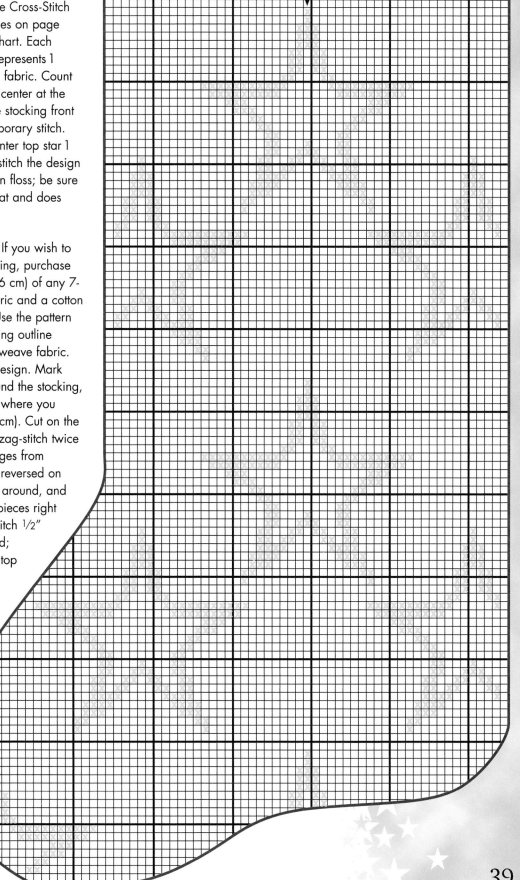

"egg"-ceptional angels

take a crack at these cute and unusual ornaments for the tree. mother-of-pearl or gold-crackle foil is applied to blown-out eggshells, while gold corkscrew icicles form a quirky halo. hang them on your tree, or display them in a nest as shown.

Materials

FOR EACH ANGEL
- Egg
- Chenille stem
- Black dimensional paint
- Permanent-ink fine-line markers: black, pink
- Pink acrylic paint
- Foiling kit: mother-of-pearl and abalone, gold crackle

- 6" (15 cm) gold metallic thread
- Gold corkscrew metallic foil icicles, thin metallic thread or fine-mesh metal kitchen scrubber
- Small ribbon rose
- 2¼" (6 cm) purchased angel wings, or make from craft foam or felt
- Miscellaneous items: sewing needle, paint palette, small foam block, cotton swab, scissors, white craft glue

1. *Blowing Egg:* Poke a hole in both ends of the egg, which must be at room temperature. Carefully blow out the egg. Wash the shell and let it dry.

2. *Handle:* Insert the chenille stem into the hole at the small end of the egg to use as a handle while you work. When not working, insert the other end of the stem into the foam block.

3. *Face:* Refer to the photo throughout. Use the black dimensional paint to dot the eyes. Use the black marker to draw the eyelashes and the pink marker to draw the mouth and dot the nose; see the Step 3 illustration. Let the paint and inks dry completely. Use a cotton swab to gently rub a tiny amount of pink paint onto each cheek.

4. *Foiling:* Refer to the manufacturer's instructions to apply foil to the entire egg. If using the gold crackle kit, do not cover the face.

5. *Hanging Loop:* Remove the chenille stem. Knot the ends of gold metallic thread together. See the Step 5 illustration to apply glue to the knot and carefully push the knot into the hole on top of the egg. Let the glue dry.

6. *Hair:* Stretch a length of corkscrew icicles to loosen the curl. Fold the length several times, then tie the center with gold thread. See the Step 6 illustration to arrange the hair as desired and glue to the angel's head. Let the glue dry, then shape the hair.

7. *Finishing:* Glue a ribbon rose to the head and the wings to the center back.

Ribbon wreaths

Materials

FOR BOTH WREATHS
- Jewelry adhesive
- 12" (30.5 cm) wire for hanging loop

FOR LARGE WREATH
- Tools: small handsaw, fine sandpaper
- 10" (25.5 cm) wooden embroidery hoop
- 1 yd. (0.95 m) each gold wire-edged ribbon: 1" (2.5 cm), 1⅝" (4 cm), 2½" (6.5 cm) and 3¾" (9.5 cm) wide
- Sprigs of ivy and gold berries

FOR SMALL WREATH
- ⅔ yd. (0.63 m) each gold wire-edged ribbon: 1" (2.5 cm) and 1½" (3.8 cm) wide
- 12" (30.5 cm) of 16-gauge wire and gold cord
- 4 pink ribbon roses, 5 pink ribbon rosebuds
- Miscellaneous items: straight pins, tape measure, pencil, sewing machine and matching threads, masking tape, sewing needle, wire cutters, scissors

easy, elegant wreaths don't have to be made of greens or florals. here are two made of ribbon layers, stitched together and gathered on hoops of wood or wire.

Large Wreath

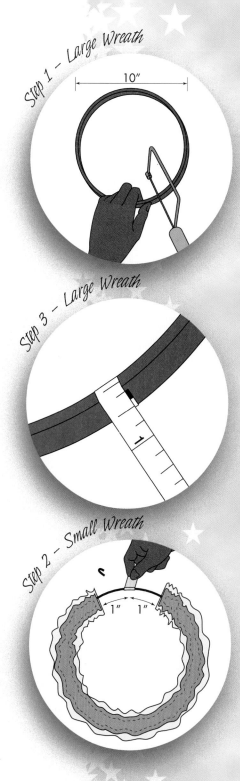

10"

1 *Base*: See the Step 1 illustration to saw an opening in the inner embroidery hoop at any spot. Sand the ends smooth. Set aside or throw away the outer hoop.

2 *Layering*: Place the widest ribbon on a flat work surface. Center the 2½" (6.5 cm) ribbon over the widest ribbon, tucking under ¼" (6 mm) on the short ends. Repeat to layer the 1" (2.5 cm) ribbon on top, and pin all 3 ribbon layers together. The 1⅝" (4 cm) ribbon will be used for the wreath bow.

3 *Ribbon Pocket*: Measure around the wooden hoop, as shown in the Step 3 illustration. Divide this measurement by 2, and add ⅛" (3 mm) for ease. If a hoop measures ⅝" (1.5 cm) around, half would be ⁵⁄₁₆" (7.5 mm). Adding ⅛" (3 mm) would make a ⁷⁄₁₆" (1.2 cm) pocket. Stitch 2 rows of straight stitches centered widthwise down the middle of the 3 layered ribbons. Make the rows as far apart as the width you calculated; backstitch at both ends.

4 *Gathering*: Insert 1 end of the wooden hoop into the stitched ribbon pocket; gather the ribbon onto the hoop. Work the ribbon all the way around, leaving 1" (2.5 cm) of hoop open on both ends. Use masking tape to tape the hoop together at the cut. Push the ribbon ends together over the masking tape, and distribute the gathers evenly around the hoop to form a wreath.

1" 1"

5 *Bow*: Tie a simple 2-loop bow, as shown in the photo. Place the bow over the spot where the hoop was joined, covering the wreath ribbon ends; glue at the center knot. Arrange the streamers as desired, and spot-glue them to the wreath.

6 *Finishing*: Use a sewing needle to insert the wire for the hanging loop through the ribbon on the back side of the wreath. Adjust the loop to the desired length, make a knot, and trim the ends. Glue the ivy sprigs and gold berries as shown in the photo.

Small Wreath

1 *Gathering*: Repeat Step 2 of Large Wreath to layer the narrow ribbon over the wider ribbon. Stitch 2 rows ⅜" (1 cm) apart through the 2 layers of ribbons. Bend back ½" (1.3 cm) of wire on 1 end. Shape the wire into a circle; insert the bent end into the stitched ribbon pocket, gathering the ribbon onto the wire circle. Work the ribbon all the way around, leaving 1" (2.5 cm) open on both ends.

2 *Finishing*: See the Step 2 illustration to cut off the bent wire. Use masking tape to tape the wire ends together. Push the ribbon ends together over the masking tape, and distribute the gathers evenly around the wire to form a wreath. Repeat Step 6 of Large Wreath to make the hanging loop and decorate with roses, rosebuds and gold cord bow.

Oriental star
ornament

Simply stringing beads and sequins in interesting combinations turns a tea ball into a dazzling star.

Materials

- Large oval aluminum tea ball. Tea balls come with many different hole designs; it should have 2-4 rows of holes on the lid and at least 5 rows of holes on the bottom.
- Silver sequins, 1 package each: 8 mm, 10 mm
- 1/4 yd. (0.25 m) silver double loop braid, 1/2" (1.3 cm) wide
- 4 mm faceted crystal beads, four
- 6 mm faceted beads: 200 crystal, 260 light blue

- 10 mm saucer iridescent blue beads, 55
- 12 mm light blue berry bead
- 4 mm round silver beads, 480
- 3 x 6 mm silver oval pearl beads, 20
- No. 11 beading (flexible) needle
- Beading thread
- Miscellaneous items: scissors, ruler, pliers, heavy-duty adhesive

1   *Lid Preparation:* Remove chain from the lid with the pliers, being careful not to bend lid. Save the large hook, and discard remainder of chain. Cut 2 yd. (1.85 m) of beading thread. Attach a 4 mm crystal bead at 1 end with a triple knot, leaving a 3" (7.5 cm) tail. Thread other end through needle. Run needle through center hole of lid from inside to outside. Apply dot of glue to secure knot.

2 *Hanging Loop:* Thread all sequins curved side down. Thread needle with 10 mm sequin, a 6 mm blue bead, the berry bead, a 6 mm blue bead, and 4 round silver beads. Run needle through loop end of large hook, and add 4 more round silver beads. Run needle back through faceted and berry beads to inside of lid.

Step 3

3 *Lid Top Row:* Insert needle up through hole of next row. Thread needle with 8 mm sequin, 6 mm blue bead, and a silver round bead. Run needle back through 6 mm bead and sequin and to inside of lid; repeat around row, keep the thread tight, but loop the end over a finger, as shown in the Step 3 illustration, to prevent it from tangling. Run needle up through first set of beads in row. Going through round beads, add a silver oval pearl bead between each group. Insert needle down through first set of beads to inside of lid.

4 *Lid Middle Row:* Skip 1 row of holes, if tea ball lid has 4 rows of holes. If tea ball lid has 2 rows of holes, do Step 5 first, omitting the first 8 mm sequin. Then go back around the holes and do Step 4. If tea ball lid has 3 rows of holes, begin here. Insert needle up through hole in next row. Thread needle with 8 mm sequin, 6 mm blue bead, and a silver round bead, then insert needle back through beads to inside of lid. Repeat around row.

5 *Lid Bottom Row:* Bring needle up through hole in last row of lid and thread with 8 mm sequin, silver oval pearl bead, silver round bead, saucer bead, and silver round bead. Run needle back through oval pearl bead, sequin and top of lid, being careful not to pull thread too tight. Leave about 3/8" (1 cm) of thread between the hole and the top oval bead so beads will hang down slightly over edge.

Bottom Beading Guide

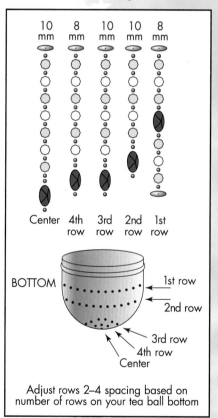

10 mm	8 mm	10 mm	10 mm	8 mm
Center	4th row	3rd row	2nd row	1st row

BOTTOM — 1st row, 2nd row, 3rd row, 4th row, Center

Adjust rows 2–4 spacing based on number of rows on your tea ball bottom

6 *Finishing Lid:* Tie remaining thread to beginning tail and make a triple knot. Glue knot to top of lid, and clip remaining thread. Glue silver braid to lid sides, overlapping ends. Trim excess.

7 *Center Bottom:* Refer to Step 1 to cut 3 yd. (2.75 m) of beading thread and attach to center bottom of ball. Refer to Bottom Beading Guide for the center and rows 1–4. Thread needle with 10 mm sequin and silver round bead. Beginning and ending with a blue bead, alternately add four 6 mm blue and three 6 mm crystal beads to strand, separating each with silver round bead. To this strand add 2 silver round beads, a saucer bead, and a silver round bead. Thread needle back through beads, starting with first silver round bead after last faceted bead.

8 *Bottom: 4th Row:* Bring needle up through next row and repeat Step 7, starting with an 8 mm sequin, and using 3 of each color of faceted beads. *3rd Row:* Space out the 3 remaining rows evenly over the number of rows on tea ball bottom, with the 1st row in the top row of holes. Repeat the Bottom 4th Row, beginning with a 10 mm sequin. *2nd Row:* Repeat the Bottom 4th Row, leaving off last crystal faceted bead. *1st Row:* Thread needle with an 8 mm sequin and silver round bead. Add the following beads, separating each with a silver round bead: blue bead, crystal bead, blue bead, saucer bead, blue bead, crystal bead, and blue bead. End with a silver round bead and 8 mm sequin. Thread needle back through beads; continue around row. Refer to Step 6 to tie off thread.

Heavenly tabletop

Set a celestial table with a gold- and silver-leaf-embossed centerpiece and candleholders, while metallic paint adds shine to the table linens.

Materials

FOR BOTH PROJECTS
- Paintbrushes: No. 1 liner; Nos. 4 and 10 flat; two 1" (2.5 cm) sponges
- Pattern Sheet

FOR ANGEL CENTERPIECE & STAR CANDLEHOLDERS
- 1' x 4' (0.32 x 1.27 m) 3/4" (2 cm) pine wood
- Bandsaw, jigsaw or scroll saw
- 1 1/2" x 1" (3.8 x 2.5 cm) wood candle cup, two
- Oil paints: black, burnt alizarin, metallic gold, metallic silver, burgundy
- Acrylic paints: white, burnt sienna, cadmium red light, alizarin crimson, black
- Gesso
- Polyurethane gloss varnish
- 25 squares silver and gold leaf, 5" (12.5 cm) wide
- Gold-leaf adhesive and clean, dry, soft 1" (2.5 cm) paintbrush
- Four 1 1/4" (3.2 cm) wood screws

FOR ANGELIC TABLE LINENS
- White cotton/linen blend placemat and matching napkin, desired number
- Fabric paints: white, black, metallic gold, metallic silver, vermilion, brown, iridescent white
- Miscellaneous items: pencil, tracing and graphite paper, paint palette, turpentine, tack cloth, medium and fine sandpaper, paper towels, white transfer paper, soft cloth, old toothbrush, screwdriver, drill and bit, stylus, 12" (30.5 cm) square cardboard, press cloth, iron, masking tape

Angel Centerpiece & Star Candleholders

1 *Preparation:* Trace the patterns onto tracing paper. Trace onto pine as shown in the Step 1 illustration along with a 3" x 9½" (7.5 x 24.3 cm) base. Use a saw to cut out the 5 pieces. Sand pieces and candle cups with medium, then fine sandpaper and remove dust with tack cloth. Use a sponge brush to basecoat all wood pieces with gesso; let dry. Sand lightly and remove dust with tack cloth. Basecoat all wood pieces with burgundy using a sponge brush; let dry.

Step 1 - Angel Centerpiece & Star Candleholders

2 *Adhesive:* Brush a thin coat of leaf adhesive over burgundy paint with 1" (2.5 cm) sponge brush; follow manufacturer's instructions to let it set about 1 hour. Cut leaf sheets into 2½" (6.5 cm) squares. Pick up a leaf square, holding it between the tissues; oils from your hand will leave marks. Place on surface, sliding bottom tissue away; press into place on adhesive. Remove tissue; use soft brush to tamp, adhering leaf to surface. Then smooth it out with brush strokes as shown in the Step 2 illustration.

3 *Foiling:* Apply leaf to entire surface, randomly overlapping some sheets and leaving small cracks between others to let burgundy paint show through. Apply gold leaf to the 3 stars, and silver leaf to the wings, halo, base and candle cups. Let dry 24 hours. Brush off any excess leaf with soft brush; save pieces for future use, if desired. Apply a coat of varnish over all foiled surfaces.

Step 2 - Angel Centerpiece & Star Candleholders

4 *Antiquing:* Mix black oil paint, varnish and a little turpentine to make a transparent ink-like glaze. Use the No. 10 flat brush to coat the foiled areas on the angel. Wipe off excess with soft cloth. Mix a glaze of burnt alizarin, varnish and a little turpentine, and brush on the angel's dress. Wipe off lightly, leaving the edges darker. See page 160 for Painting Instructions and Techniques. Use a No. 10 flat brush and burnt alizarin to shade the dress ruffles. Let dry 24 hours.

5 *Face:* Use transfer paper to transfer face details and stars to the wood. Paint the face details with acrylics. Mix white, cadmium red light and burnt sienna to make peach, and basecoat the face and hands with the No. 4 brush. Use burnt sienna to shade the face along the hairline, around the eyes and nose, under the chin and at the wrists. Use the liner brush and burnt sienna to outline the eyes, nose, chin and hands. Shade the cheeks with alizarin crimson and a touch of cadmium red light. See the Step 5 illustration to use the liner brush to paint the lips alizarin crimson, the eyes white, the iris burnt sienna and the pupils black. Use white to highlight cheeks, nose and chin, and each eye at the 11 o'clock and 5 o'clock marks. Use burnt sienna to paint the eyelashes, eyebrows, lips and cheek outline, and basecoat the hair. Use the liner brush and black to paint the hair details.

Step 5 - Angel Centerpiece & Star Candleholders

6 *Finishing:* Use oil metallic gold to paint the stars on the wings and silver to paint the star necklace and the stars on the dress. Spatter-paint all areas except the face with the black ink-like glaze and the toothbrush. Let dry. Seal all pieces with several coats of varnish.

(Continued)

7 *Assembly:* Find and mark the center of the candleholder stars, candle cups, angel bottom, wings and base. Drill through the marked holes, as shown in the Step 7 illustration. Insert a screw into the back of the wings. Place wings behind the angel, referring to the photo, and screw into the angel's back. Insert screws from the bottom of the base and stars, and screw in the holes on the angel bottom and candle cups, respectively.

Step 7 - Angel Centerpiece & Star Candleholders

Angelic Table Linens

1 *Preparation:* Trace the patterns to tracing paper. Use a stylus and graphite paper to lightly transfer the angel pattern to a napkin corner and the star pattern to opposite corners of a placemat; do not do angel details yet. Cover cardboard with paper towels. Tape napkin or placemat to cardboard with masking tape while painting.

2 *Angel Basecoat:* Refer to page 160 for Painting Instructions and Techniques; let dry between each color and coat. Use the No. 10 flat brush to basecoat the wings and halo with silver, the dress and star above head with gold, and the liner brush to paint the hair with brown. Mix white with a little vermilion and brown; paint the hands and face with 2 coats. Transfer face details and stars to angel.

Step 3 - Angelic Table Linens

Step 5 - Angelic Table Linens

3 *Shading & Highlighting:* Use the No. 4 flat brush to shade the wings and halo with black and silver; see the Step 3 illustration. Mix vermilion and brown and refer to the photo to shade the edge of the dress and ruffles. Use gold to blend shading into the dress and iridescent white to highlight the ruffles. Use the liner brush and brown to shade the face along the hairline, around eyes and nose, under the chin and on wrists, and to outline the eyes, nose, chin and hands.

4 *Face:* Use vermilion to shade the cheeks and paint the lips. Use white to paint the eyes; paint brown irises and black pupils. Use a dash of white to highlight the cheeks, nose and chin, and each eye at 11 o'clock and 5 o'clock marks. Paint the eyelashes, eyebrows and outline lips and cheeks brown.

5 *Finishing:* Use the liner brush and black to define the linework. Use gold to paint the stars on the wings and silver to paint the star necklace and star buttons on the dress, as shown in the Step 5 illustration.

6 *Placemats:* Use the No. 4 flat brush and gold to paint the large star, and the liner brush and silver to paint the small stars. To heat-set napkins and placemats, follow fabric paint manufacturer's instructions or cover painted areas with a press cloth and press with a medium-hot iron for 1 minute.

My true Love
gave to me

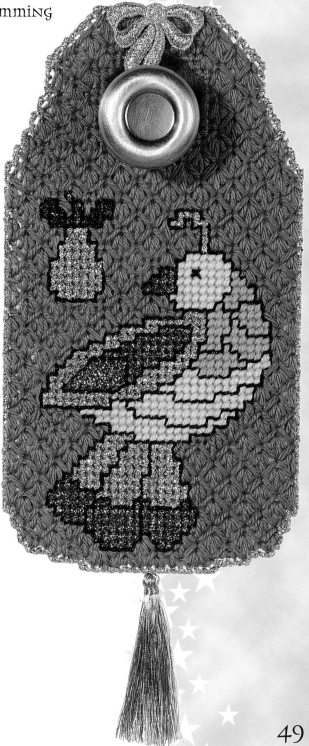

Hang this gilded partridge stitched on plastic canvas on any door in your home for an elegant seasonal touch. every time you pass by, you'll start humming that happy tune.

Materials

- ½ sheet 7-mesh plastic canvas
- Worsted-weight yarn: 22 yd. (20.24 m) teal blue, 4 yd. (3.7 m) lt. beige, 2 yd. (1.85 m) med. beige
- Metallic plastic canvas yarn: 7-count: 10 yd. (9.15 m) gold, 4 yd. (3.7 m) copper, 1 yd. (0.95 m) forest green; 10-count: 10 yd. (9.15 m) black
- No. 16 tapestry needle
- Gold trims: 3" (7.5 cm) metallic tassel, 1¾" (4.5 cm) embroidered bow appliqué
- Pattern Page 166
- Miscellaneous items: scissors, hot glue gun

 1 *Preparation:* Refer to the Plastic Canvas General Instructions and Stitches on page 159 and the Stitch Chart on page 166. Use scissors to cut a 38x69-bar piece of plastic canvas. Follow the bold outline on the Stitch Chart to carefully cut out the door hanger shape. Each line on the chart represents 1 bar of plastic canvas.

2 *Stitching:* Use the 7-count metallic yarns and beige yarns to work the pear and partridge designs in continental stitches (and copper straight stitches on the wing) in the colors shown on the Stitch Chart. Stitch the partridge's topknot with gold cross-stitches. Fill in the background with teal blue modified leaf stitches. Backstitch as shown with the 10-count metallic black; make the cross-stitch eye over the continental stitch.

3 *Finishing:* Overcast the outer edges with gold, and the inner doorknob edge with teal blue. Hot-glue appliquéd bow to center top, and tassel to center bottom.

THE NORTH POLE

With the help of his flying reindeer, jolly ol' St. Nick brings his sleigh full of gifts, candies, and toys to good girls and boys (and the family pet, too).

Santa in the sky
vest

Who would have thought that, after all that reindeer and sleigh time, santa likes to hang out in the sky on his day off?

Materials

- Adult-size antique white felt vest
- Felt: 5" (12.5 cm) square gold, 6" (15 cm) square each antique white and wheat, 8" (20.5 cm) square each denim and black, 12" (30.5 cm) square cranberry
- ¼ yd. (0.25 m) paper-backed fusible web
- Embroidery floss: Ecru, Black No. 310, Navy Blue No. 336, Medium Topaz No. 783, Dk. Garnet No. 814
- Four ⅛" (3 mm) black flat buttons
- ⅓ yd. (0.32 m) ⅛" 3 mm) burgundy ribbon
- Miscellaneous items: tracing paper, pencil, scissors, iron, press cloth or pressing paper, embroidery needle

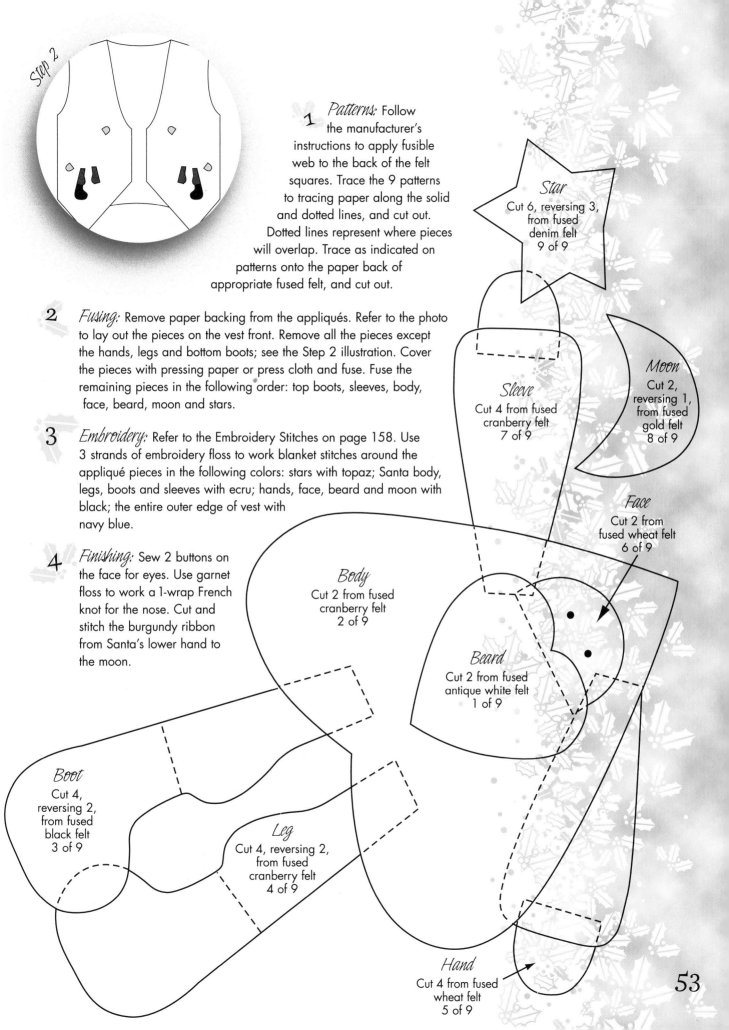

Step 2

1 *Patterns:* Follow the manufacturer's instructions to apply fusible web to the back of the felt squares. Trace the 9 patterns to tracing paper along the solid and dotted lines, and cut out. Dotted lines represent where pieces will overlap. Trace as indicated on patterns onto the paper back of appropriate fused felt, and cut out.

2 *Fusing:* Remove paper backing from the appliqués. Refer to the photo to lay out the pieces on the vest front. Remove all the pieces except the hands, legs and bottom boots; see the Step 2 illustration. Cover the pieces with pressing paper or press cloth and fuse. Fuse the remaining pieces in the following order: top boots, sleeves, body, face, beard, moon and stars.

3 *Embroidery:* Refer to the Embroidery Stitches on page 158. Use 3 strands of embroidery floss to work blanket stitches around the appliqué pieces in the following colors: stars with topaz; Santa body, legs, boots and sleeves with ecru; hands, face, beard and moon with black; the entire outer edge of vest with navy blue.

4 *Finishing:* Sew 2 buttons on the face for eyes. Use garnet floss to work a 1-wrap French knot for the nose. Cut and stitch the burgundy ribbon from Santa's lower hand to the moon.

Star
Cut 6, reversing 3, from fused denim felt
9 of 9

Moon
Cut 2, reversing 1, from fused gold felt
8 of 9

Sleeve
Cut 4 from fused cranberry felt
7 of 9

Face
Cut 2 from fused wheat felt
6 of 9

Body
Cut 2 from fused cranberry felt
2 of 9

Beard
Cut 2 from fused antique white felt
1 of 9

Boot
Cut 4, reversing 2, from fused black felt
3 of 9

Leg
Cut 4, reversing 2, from fused cranberry felt
4 of 9

Hand
Cut 4 from fused wheat felt
5 of 9

Loaded With gifts

a wooden sleigh loaded with colorful packages makes a festive accent for the holiday table. the gift boxes are merely wooden blocks that have been painted and decorated with metallic confetti shapes and tinsel.

Materials

- 8³⁄₈" x 5" x 4¹⁄₄" (21.5 x 12.5 x 10.8 cm) wooden sleigh*
- 2 each wooden shapes, ¹⁄₈" (3 mm) thick*: 2¹⁄₄" (6 cm) deer, 2" (5 cm) deer, 1" (2.5 cm) star
- Wooden blocks*: three 1" (2.5 cm), two 1¹⁄₄" (3.2 cm), two 1¹⁄₂" (3.8 cm), one 1³⁄₄" (4.5 cm)
- Wood sealer
- Metallic acrylic craft paints: green, blue, gold, silver
- Acrylic craft paints: red
- Paintbrushes: 1" (2.5 cm) sponge, ¹⁄₂" (1.3 cm) flat, fine liner

- High-gloss finish
- Metallic confetti: stars, circles, etc.
- ¹⁄₈" (3 mm) tinsel: red, green, silver
- Gold elastic cord
- Fresh or dried greens
- Pattern Sheet
- Miscellaneous items: extra-fine sandpaper, tack cloth, paint palette, tracing and yellow transfer paper, pencil, ballpoint pen, thick white craft glue, toothpick

*(See Sources on pg. 176 for purchasing information.)

Step 3

1 **Preparation:** Sand all the wooden pieces until smooth. Remove dust with tack cloth. Use the sponge brush to apply 1 coat of wood sealer, following manufacturer's instructions. Sand and remove dust again.

2 **Basecoating:** Refer to the Painting Instructions and Techniques on page 160. Let paints and finishes dry between colors and coats. Use the flat brush to basecoat all sides of the sleigh with red, and the reindeer and stars with metallic gold. Use the flat brush to basecoat the wooden blocks with the paints as follows:

1" (2.5 cm)	Silver, blue	1¹⁄₄" (3.2 cm)	Silver, gold
1¹⁄₂" (3.8 cm)	Blue, green, red	1³⁄₄" (4.5 cm)	Red

Apply at least 2 coats of paint to all wooden pieces; use as many coats as necessary to cover completely to your satisfaction. Use the sponge brush to apply high-gloss finish to all the painted wooden pieces.

Step 5

3 **Pattern:** Trace the scroll pattern to tracing paper twice, reversing 1. Cut a piece of yellow transfer paper 2" (5 cm) wide and the width of the sleigh. See the Step 3 illustration to place the transfer paper on the sleigh, and place the scroll pattern over it. Use a pen to transfer the pattern to both sides of the sleigh.

4 **Sleigh Decorations:** Use the liner brush to paint the scroll with metallic gold. Use the craft glue to glue 2 reindeer and 1 star to each side of the sleigh; refer to the photo.

Step 6

5 **Packages:** Refer to the photo to glue the metallic confetti shapes to the wooden blocks, or as desired. Use a toothpick to apply the glue, as shown in the Step 5 illustration. Glue tinsel strips diagonally on packages to look like striped paper.

6 **Finishing:** Tie tinsel around packages for a ribbon, tie ends in a knot, and trim. See the Step 6 illustration to use scissors to curl another matching piece of tinsel. Dot the top of a package with glue, and place the curly tinsel bow in it. Tie gold elastic cord around other packages. Load the presents in the sleigh, and add desired greenery.

HeirLoom
Globes

Reminiscent of winter snow globes,
these victorian-inspired versions are a perfect showcase for
a cherished family keepsake, collectible or antique.

Materials

FOR BOTH GLOBES

- Glass light fixture globe: 8" (20.5 cm) for Santa globe, 6" (15 cm) for doll globe
- Mauve acrylic craft paint, 1/2" (1.3 cm) sponge brush
- Round wood disk or plaque: 10" (25.5 cm) for Santa globe, 8" (20.5 cm) for doll globe
- Porcelain heirloom or keepsake: 6" (15 cm) Santa with toy pack or doll
- Decorations: mini packages, Christmas balls, dried flowers, pinecones, berry sprays, etc.
- Miniature artificial pine garland: 24" (61 cm) for Santa globe, 18" (46 cm) for doll globe

- 1 yd. (0.95 m) decorative ribbon: 2 coordinating 1 1/2" (3.8 cm) wide for Santa globe, 1/2" (1.3 cm) wide for doll globe

FOR SANTA GLOBE

- 3" (7.5 cm) Styrofoam® ball
- 6" (15 cm) small wood dowel
- 7" (18 cm) circle tapestry fabric
- 1/2 yd. (0.5 m) decorative braid

FOR DOLL GLOBE

- 6" (15 cm) miniature topiary tree
- Miscellaneous items: serrated knife, low-temp glue gun, scissors, ruler, wire cutters, 26-gauge craft wire

Santa Globe

1. *Preparation:* Use the sponge brush to paint the wood disk mauve; use as many coats as necessary to cover completely. Use hot glue gun for all gluing.

2. *Base:* Cut Styrofoam ball in half with serrated knife. Glue 1 half to center of wood disk. Insert dowel into center of ball as a stand for Santa.

3. *Fabric Covering:* Cut a slit in the fabric circle from 1 edge to the center. Position fabric over ball, overlapping slit, and glue in place, as shown in the Step 3 illustration. Glue decorative braid over the raw edges of the fabric circle.

4. *Santa Heirloom:* Glue Santa to dowel. Add any special miniatures or decorations such as toys in his pack, a wreath over his wrist and packages in his arms. Slip globe over the arrangement; glue to the base, if desired.

5. *Embellishing:* Arrange the pine garland around the edge of the wood base. See the Step 5 illustration to cut the excess garland; glue garland in place. Arrange and glue dried flowers, packages, miniatures and other decorations onto the pine garland. Make a multi-loop bow from each ribbon, and twist wire tightly around the center. Trim excess wire, and glue, 1 on top of the other, to the pine garland.

Doll Globe

1. *Preparation:* Repeat Step 1 of Santa globe. Glue miniature topiary tree onto the painted wooden disk, slightly off center, as shown in the Step 1 illustration. Glue doll to the topiary tree.

2. *Finishing:* Add packages, miniatures and other decorations around base of tree and doll. Slip globe over the arrangement; glue to the base, if desired. Repeat Step 5 of Santa Globe to finish the doll globe.

Pampered pet stockings

too cute to be missed,

santa wiLL fiLL these pampered pet stockings, fused with fabric dog bones and mice, to the tip-top with tasty treats.

Materials

FOR BOTH STOCKINGS

- 45" (115 cm) fabrics: 1/4 yd. (0.25 m) single-side quilted muslin, 3/8 yd. (0.35 m) red Christmas print, 1/8 yd. (0.15 m) green Christmas print, 1/8 yd. (0.15 m) cream print, 3" x 6" (7.5 x 15 cm) medium gray broadcloth
- 1/4 yd. (0.25 m) paper-backed fusible web
- 1 pkg. green corded piping
- Embroidery floss: black, dark gray
- Three 6 mm black pom-poms
- Red satin ribbon: 1/2 yd. (0.5 m) of 1/8" (3 mm); 1/3 yd. (0.32 m) of 1" (2.5 cm)
- White craft glue
- Pattern Sheet
- Miscellaneous items: tracing paper, pencil, scissors, ruler, straight pins, sewing machine and matching threads, iron, sewing needle, black ultra-fine-point permanent-ink marker

1 *Patterns & Cutting:* Trace the patterns to tracing paper, and cut out. Cut out stockings and linings as indicated on stocking pattern. Cut a 2½" x 11½" (6.5 x 29.3 cm) cuff from red print for the dog stocking or cream print for the cat stocking. Cut a 1½" x 4½" (3.8 x 11.5 cm) piece from cream and a 1½" x 9" (3.8 x 23 cm) piece each from red and green print fabrics for dog bones. Cut a 1½" x 7½" (3.8 x 19.3 cm) piece from red print and a 1½" x 4½" (3.8 x 11.5 cm) piece from green print for stars. Sew all seams right sides together using a ¼" (6 mm) seam allowance.

2 *Piping:* Refer to the Step 2A illustration to pin and sew piping around edge of each stocking front and along 1 long edge of each cuff on right side of fabric. Clip piping along curves. See the Step 2B illustration to turn piping back and topstitch.

3 *Fusing:* Follow manufacturer's instructions to fuse web to wrong side of the following fabrics: dog bone fabrics, gray broadcloth and red and green star prints. Trace bone, star and mice patterns onto paper backing of appropriate fused fabrics; cut out. Peel off paper backings.

 Cuffs: Stitch all seams right sides together, using a ¼" (6 mm) seam allowance. Fold cuff right sides together, matching short edges, and pin. Stitch short edges, and turn right side out. Center and fuse large cream bone to red print dog cuff with cuff seam at right. See the Step 4 illustration to use marker to write name on bone and draw small quilting lines around bone. With seam at right, use black marker to write cat's name centered. Fuse a red star to each side of name.

5 *Dog Stocking:* Refer to the photo to fuse red and green bones to stocking front. Refer to the Embroidery Stitches on page 158 for long stitch and backstitch. Use 2 strands of black floss to sew irregular long stitches around bone edges.

6 *Cat Stocking:* Refer to the photo to fuse stars and mice to stocking front. Use marker to dot eyes on mice. Use 2 strands of black floss to sew irregular long stitches around star edges. Use 2 strands of gray floss to backstitch tails on mice. Cut ⅛" (3 mm) ribbon into 3 pieces, and tie small bows. Glue a bow and a pom-pom nose on each mouse.

7 *Stocking Assembly:* With right sides facing, stitch muslin stocking fronts and backs together; turn right side out. With right sides facing, sew lining stockings together; do not turn right side out. See the Step 7 illustration to insert lining in muslin stocking. Match seams and stitch ⅛" (3 mm) in along top edge. Cut 6" (15 cm) of 1" (2.5 cm) ribbon; fold in half and stitch to inside top back seam of stocking for hanger. Turn cuff wrong side out and insert in stocking, matching seams. Sew top seam, and turn right side out.

Step 2

11½"

2½"

Cat cuff   A

Cat cuff   B

Step 4

Cuff seam

MAGGIE

Step 7

Lining, wrong side out

Stocking, right side out

Handmade paper gift tags

A COMBINATION OF HANDMADE PAPER, WHITE TULLE AND DRIED FLOWERS makes for a charming gift tag, WHICH NOT ONLY LOOKS GREAT, BUT SMELLS GREAT TOO. WITHOUT THE SECOND LAYER FOR WRITING ON, THESE TAGS CAN ALSO DOUBLE AS CHRISTMAS ORNAMENTS.

Materials

FOR EACH GIFT TAG

- 6" (15 cm) pieces of handmade paper, 3 red for heart, 2 red and 1 white for star, 2 lt. green and 1 dk. green for wreath—available in craft and art supply stores
- 12" (30.5 cm) deckled-edge ruler
- 1" (2.5 cm) sponge brush
- 6" (15 cm) white tulle

- Dried florals: hydrangea petals, lavender, baby's breath
- 1/8" (3 mm) hole punch
- 24" (61 cm) gold cord for hanging loop and bow
- Pattern Pages 168-169
- Miscellaneous items: tracing paper, pencil, straight pins, sewing needle, scissors, sewing machine with gold metallic thread

Step 2

1 *Pattern:* Trace the patterns to tracing paper, and cut out. Place pattern on the appropriate color of handmade paper indicated on the pattern, and trace around it very lightly onto the paper with pencil. Cut out the shapes from paper, **making them about 1" (2.5 cm) larger than pattern.**

2 *Dampening:* Put water into a small bowl; place shape on a flat waterproof work surface. Dampen the edge of a shape 3/4" (2 cm) in from the edges with the sponge brush dipped in water, as shown in the Step 2 illustration. Edges should just be damp, not soggy. Let set for about 1 minute. To make a smaller top layer, such as the white star, dampen the edge 1" (2.5 cm) in, right to the traced line.

Step 3

3 *Deckled Edges:* Place the deckled-edge ruler along the damp edge of the paper shape. Hold down the ruler firmly, and slowly tear the paper up along the ruler edge to give it a soft edge. Move the ruler over, and continue tearing along the shape; see the Step 3 illustration. When the shape is completed, remove the ruler and smooth the edges down and flat. Let the paper dry completely.

4 *Dried Florals:* Arrange the desired dried florals onto the top handmade paper shapes; break the lavender and baby's breath sprigs into small pieces. The wreath has hydrangea petals only; the star, hydrangea and baby's breath; and the heart has lavender and baby's breath.

Step 6

5 *Stitching:* Layer a piece of tulle over the dried florals. Pin the tulle in place in a few spots. Machine-stitch along the edge of the paper with gold metallic thread. Use a straight stitch on the heart, a zigzag stitch on the star, and the multistitch-zigzag on the wreath. Set your machine for a little longer stitch than usual. Trim the tulle close to the stitching.

6 *Bows:* Layer the stitched shape with tulle and dried florals over the plain paper shape. Use the hole punch to make 2 holes about 1/2" (1.3 cm) apart at the top. Make 2 more holes in the heart near the bottom. See the Step 6A illustration to thread the gold cord onto a needle and run a few times around the holes; tie in a bow. Use the rest of the gold cord to run through the holes to make a hanging loop. Write the message on the second layer; see Step 6B.

61

CROCHET Bearded Santa ornament

Combining two favorite crafts, painting and crochet, this crochet bearded santa is a real charmer.

Materials

- Wood: 1/4" (6 mm) pine, 5" (12.5 cm) square; 1/4" (6 mm) dowel, 1/4" (6 mm) long
- Scroll saw
- Acrylic paints: red, white, peach
- Paintbrushes: 1/4" (6 mm) flat, fine liner
- 25 yd. (23 m) No. 10 white cotton crochet thread
- No. 8 steel crochet hook
- 1/2" (1.3 cm) gold jingle bell
- Flat white buttons: one 3/4" (2 cm), eight 3/8" (1 cm)
- 6" (15 cm) gold cord
- Small screw eye
- Thick white craft glue
- Miscellaneous items: tracing paper, pencil, graphite paper, stylus, fine sandpaper, tack cloth, fine-point black permanent-ink marker, wedge-shaped makeup sponge, paper towels, iron, two cloth towels, large-eyed sewing needle, scissors

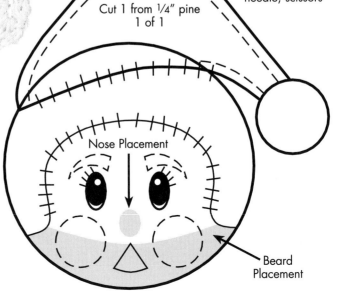

Head
Cut 1 from 1/4" pine
1 of 1

Nose Placement

Beard Placement

1 *Wood:* Trace the head pattern, and trace onto wood. Use saw to cut from wood. Sand smooth; remove dust with tack cloth. Sand 1 end of dowel round for nose. Use the graphite paper and the stylus to transfer the fur trim/hairlines and the nose placement. Glue nose to head.

2 *Basecoat:* Refer to the pattern and photo to use the flat brush to basecoat the hat red, the face peach and the fur trim white. Extend paint colors onto the edges; let dry. On the back, basecoat the hat tip white and and the remaining area red.

3 *Mouth, Cheeks & Eyebrows:* Paint mouth red. Dip the wide end of the sponge in red paint and pat on paper towels until only a little color remains. Dab on cheek area as desired; see the Step 3 illustration. Using the pointed end of the sponge, dab on white eyebrows in the same manner.

4 *Details:* Use the graphite paper and stylus to transfer all details to head. Use marker to fill in eyes and add eyelashes and stitching lines on hat. Add white highlights to eyes with liner brush.

5 *Crocheting:* Refer to the Crochet Abbreviations and Stitches on page 162. *Pattern Stitch*, work 2 dc in next ch-1 sp holding back the last lp of each dc. Yo and pull through all 3 lps on hook; 1 pattern stitch made. To begin, ch 21.

6 *Beard: Row 1:* Dc in 3rd ch from hook, * ch 1, dc in next ch. Rep from * to end of chain. Ch 3 and turn.
Row 2: *Dc in ch-1 sp, ch 1, rep from * 7 times. Sk next ch-1 sp and ch 2 (making ch 3). Dc in next ch-1 sp, *ch 1, dc in next ch-1 sp. Rep from * to end of row. Ch 3 and turn.
Row 3: *Ch 1, work pattern st in next ch-1 sp, rep from * 7 times. Ch 1, pattern st, ch 1, pattern st in ch-3 sp, ch 1 and continue pattern st, ch 1 in each ch-1 sp to end of row. Ch 3 and turn.
Row 4: Work pattern st, ch 1 in each ch-1 sp to end of row. Ch 3 and turn.
Rows 5-15: Rep this row until the next row contains only 2 ch-1 sp(s). Then, ch 4 at end of row and turn. Join with a sl st to top of ch-3 sp at opposite end of row and fasten off leaving a 6" (15 cm) tail.

7 *Attaching Beard:* Lightly dampen beard, place between 2 towels and press with a hot iron to block. Use large-eyed needle to thread 6" (15 cm) tail through bell and stitch to beard. Glue beard to face, referring to the photo, pattern and the Step 7 illustration.

8 *Finishing:* Use needle and crochet thread to sew through holes of each button. Knot and cut threads at back. Glue large button to hat tip and remaining buttons to fur trim. Twist screw eye into top of hat. Thread gold cord through eye and knot ends, for hanger.

Step 3

Step 7

North Pole
tic-tac-toe

Painted wooden spoons go from the heat of the kitchen to the heat of competition. After a winner has been declared, they can take a much-needed break in their game board, which doubles as a storage pouch.

Materials

- 5 wooden spoons
- Acrylic paints: mocha, alizarin crimson, sand, brown, pine, cranberry
- Paintbrushes: ¼" and ⅛" (6 and 3 mm) stencil, Nos. 3 and 8 round
- Fine-point black permanent-ink marker
- ¼" (6 mm) pom-poms: 5 each beige, brown
- ¼ yd. (0.25 m) 45" (115 cm) natural cotton canvas
- Black embroidery floss
- Pattern Page 168
- Miscellaneous items: tracing and graphite paper, pencil, handsaw, fine sandpaper, tack cloth, paint palette, paper towels, white craft glue, ruler, scissors, straight pins, pinking shears, embroidery needle

64

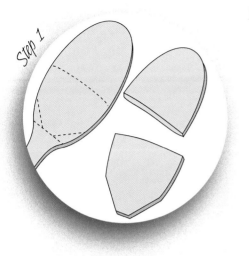

Step 1

1 *Cutting:* Refer to the Painting Instructions on page 160. Let paint dry between coats and colors. Trace the patterns onto tracing paper. Mark the dashed cutting lines on each spoon back and cut in half and cut off the handle; see the Step 1 illustration. Sand the cut edges smooth and round the bottom edge of each reindeer's face. Remove dust with a tack cloth.

2 *Patterns:* Use graphite paper and a sharp pencil to transfer the patterns to the spoon backs. Transfer the face and hat outlines to the Santa pieces and the antlers and the head outlines to the reindeer pieces. Extend the pattern lines onto the sides.

3 *Basecoating:* Use the appropriate size round brush to basecoat Santa's face with mocha, the top of his hat with alizarin crimson, and his mustache, beard, hat fur and the back of the spoon with sand. Basecoat the reindeer's head with brown, the antlers with sand, and the remainder of the spoon front and back with pine.

4 *Drybrushing:* Drybrush Santa's and the reindeers' cheeks with alizarin crimson and the ⅛" (3 mm) stencil brush. Drybrush all around the edges of each piece with cranberry and the ¼" (6 mm) stencil brush, as shown in the Step 4 illustration.

5 *Details:* Transfer the pattern details to each piece with graphite paper, or draw them in freehand. Use the pen to draw the eyes, fur details and the penstitching lines. Glue a beige pom-pom to the tip of Santa's hat and a brown pom-pom for the reindeer's nose.

6 *Marking & Cutting Game Board:* Use the ruler to lightly draw in pencil a 6¾" (17 cm) square on the canvas fabric with a ½" (1.3 cm) border around it. Mark nine 2¼" (6 cm) squares inside the large square. Fold canvas so there is a second layer behind the marked canvas, and pin all around as shown in the Step 6 illustration. Use pinking shears to cut through both layers of canvas along the marked border. Separate the layers.

7 *Game Board Assembly:* Refer to Embroidery Stitches on page 158 for how to do a running stitch. Refer to the photo to work running stitches along the inner lines and 1 outer edge of the square with 3 strands of black floss on just 1 layer of canvas. Knot the floss ends at the ends of each line on the canvas front; trim to ¼" (6 mm). Place the stitched canvas piece, faceup and matching the pinked edges, on the unstitched canvas layer. Pin around the remaining 3 outer edges of the board and work running stitches through both layers, to create a storage pocket for the game pieces; see the Step 7 illustration.

Step 4

Step 6

Step 7

Good enough
to eat

Use items that are normally just eaten during the holidays, to craft delightful home decorations. keep them for yourself, or give away as gifts; they do up so fast, you will have time for both.

Materials

FOR NUT WREATH
- 6" (15 cm) grapevine wreath
- 1 lb. (500 kg) red pistachio nuts
- 2 small pinecones
- 8" (20.5 cm) 24-gauge craft wire
- 6 strands of natural raffia, 20" (51 cm) long

FOR CANDY CANE VASE
- 14½" (36.8 cm) empty tin can
- Thirty 6" (15 cm) red/green striped candy canes
- 1 yd. (0.95 m) red grosgrain ribbon, ⅝" (1.5 cm) wide
- Miscellaneous items: hot glue gun, sandpaper or pliers

Nut Wreath

1   *Gluing:* Randomly hot-glue the pistachio nuts to the grapevine wreath, covering the front and sides; see the Step 1 illustration.

2   *Decorations:* Tie the 6 strands of raffia into a bow. Hot-glue the bow to the top center of the wreath, on the pistachios. Hot-glue the 2 pinecones below the bow, as shown in the photo.

3   *Hanging Loop:* Insert the wire through a couple of vines on the top back side of the wreath. Holding the wreath by the wire, make sure you have gone through enough vines to bear the weight of the nuts. When satisfied, twist the wire into a loop for hanging.

Candy Cane Vase

1   *Cleaning:* Completely remove the top of the tin can. Check to see that there are no sharp edges; remove by sanding or bending flat with pliers. Wash the tin can with warm soapy water to remove any food and label residue.

2   *Gluing:* Leaving the wrappers on the candy canes, hot-glue them 1 at at time around the can. See the Step 2 illustration to apply hot glue to the back side of the bottom 4" (10 cm) of the candy cane. Press the candy cane firmly onto the can, with the bottom of the candy cane slightly above the bottom of the can.

3   *Finishing:* Continue gluing the candy canes around until you meet up with the first cane and have covered the entire surface of the can. Wrap the ribbon around the candy canes, and tie a bow. Hot-glue the bow to the candy canes.

Step 1 - Nut Wreath

Step 2 - Candy Cane Vase

4"

teddy bear & stocking ornaments

easy CROSS-STITCH designs make the teddy bear and stocking great beginner projects.

Bear Ornament Stitch Chart

Stocking & Bear Ornaments Color Key

SYMBOL	DMC #	COLOR
•	—	White
x	400	Dk. Mahogany
◢	816	Garnet
T	826	Med. Blue
I	895	Vy. Dk. Hunter Green
○	3346	Hunter Green
■	3371	Black Brown
—	3371	Black Brown Backstitches

Stocking Ornament
Stitch Chart

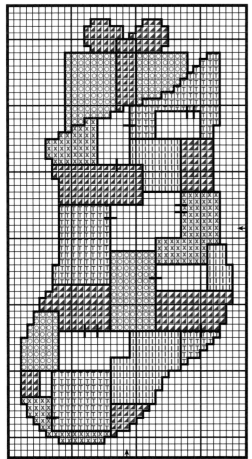

Materials

FOR BOTH ORNAMENTS

- 1 sheet 14-count natural perforated paper
- 1 skein each 6-strand embroidery floss in colors listed in the Color Key
- No. 24 tapestry needle
- 10" (25.5 cm) jute
- 7" (18 cm) square brown kraft paper
- Miscellaneous items: white craft glue, scissors

1   *Stitching:* Refer to the Perforated Plastic/Paper General Instructions and Stitches on page 159 and the Stitch Charts to cross-stitch the designs using 2 strands of floss. Each square on the chart represents 1 hole on the perforated paper. Symbols correspond to the colors in the Color Key. Use 1 strand of No. 3371 Black Brown to work all backstitches.

2   *Finishing:* Trim excess perforated paper to within 1 square of design. Glue 5" (12.5 cm) of jute to top back of ornament for hanging loop. Lightly glue kraft paper to back of ornament, covering hanging loop ends. Trim paper even with ornament edges.

christmas ornament
Quilt & pillow

for those who crave a classic look, the crossed wires quilt pattern, redone in christmas reds and greens, becomes a dazzling array of christmas ornaments, or feature a single ball on a pillow.

Materials

FOR BOTH PROJECTS

- ½ yd. (0.5 m) each 45" (115 cm) cotton print fabrics: light red, dark red, green check, dark green, white; 15" (38 cm) square for pillow back; muslin: 38" (96.5 cm) square for quilt, 15" (38 cm) square for pillow

- Low-loft batting: 38" (96.5 cm) square for quilt; 15" (38 cm) square for pillow

- Clear nylon monofilament thread

- 9" x 12" (23 x 30.5 cm) template plastic

FOR QUILT ONLY

- Extra-wide double-fold bias tape, 2 packages green

FOR PILLOW ONLY

- Natural bias corded piping

- 14" (35.5 cm) square pillow form

- Pattern Page 164

- Miscellaneous items: black fine-point permanent-ink marker, ruler, tape measure, pencil, scissors, straight pins, sewing machine and matching threads, sewing needle, iron, rotary cutter and mat (optional), masking tape, safety pins

1 *Piecing A/B/A Squares:* See the Fabric Preparation and Pattern Instructions on page 164. See the Step 1A illustration to stitch 1 white and 1 green check B to each side of a red A, and 1 white and 1 red B to each side of a green A. Make 20 red and 16 green A/B/A squares for the quilt, and 4 red A/B/A squares for the pillow. See the Step 1B illustration to stitch a white D between 2 same-colored A/B/A squares, with the white B's in the outer corners.

2 *Christmas Ornament Blocks:* See the Step 2 illustration to stitch the C squares between 2 white D's; make 5 green/white and 4 red/white C/D/C strips for the quilt, and 1 green/white strip for the pillow. Stitch the red/white C/D/C strips between the green A/B/A squares and the green/white C/D/C strips between the red A/B/A squares.

3 *Quilt Top Assembly:* Press and square off Christmas Ornament blocks; each should be 10½" (26.8 cm). Go to Step 7 to finish the pillow. Refer to the photo to stitch the 9 Christmas Ornament blocks together.

4 *Borders:* Measure quilt top across the middle. Cut 2 dark red strips that length and 2½" (6.5 cm) wide. Repeat for the side borders, measuring quilt down the middle from top to bottom. Pin-mark centers of quilt top and 4 border strips. Match the pin-marks and stitch 1 border strip each to the top and bottom edges. Stitch 2 of the green check squares to each end of the 2 remaining border strips, and stitch onto the quilt top sides; see the Step 4 illustration.

5 *Basting:* Pin-mark centers of quilt top, muslin backing, and batting. Tape backing to hard flat work surface. Begin at center, and work toward corners, stretching fabric slightly. Place batting over backing, matching at centers. Smooth, but do not stretch, working from center outward. Repeat for quilt top. Pin-baste a line up the middle of each side, starting in the center. Baste each quarter outward, placing safety pins about 5" (12.5 cm) apart. Avoid basting on seamlines. Remove tape from backing; fold backing edges over batting and quilt top to prevent raveling, and pin.

6 *Quilting & Binding:* Thread machine needle with monofilament thread and bobbin with neutral thread. Hand-quilt or machine-quilt with a walking foot, stitching-in-the ditch in all seamlines. Trim excess batting and backing to ⅜" (1 cm); baste along outer edges. Follow the bias tape manufacturer's instructions to bind the edges of the quilt, mitering the corners.

7 *Pillow:* Cut 2 each 2½" x 10½" (6.5 x 26.9 cm) and 2½" x 14½" (6.5 x 36.8 cm) dark green border strips. Pin-mark centers of the pillow top and 4 border strips. Match the pin marks and stitch the shorter strips to opposite sides of the Christmas Ornament block. Repeat to stitch the remaining border strips to the open pillow sides. Repeat Steps 5 and 6 to baste and quilt the pillow. Trim the pillow layers to 14½" (36.8 cm). Baste the piping to the pillow front, matching raw edges and right sides together. Pin the pillow back to the pillow front, right sides together, and stitch along 3 sides. Clip corners, and turn right side out. Insert the pillow form, and slipstitch the opening shut.

Step 1

A

B A B

B A B

B A D A B

B

Step 2

B A D A B

D C D

B A D A B

Step 4

71

stenciLed
Santa clock

Santa counts the hours until his christmas eve journey on this wood clock. super easy to paint, stencil and trim, it's certain to be a welcome addition to any holiday home decorating collection.

Materials

- 6½" x 10" (16.3 x 25.5 cm) wood rectangle clock
- Clock movement
- 1⅞" (4.7 cm) gold clock hands
- Acrylic paints: pale green, dark green, antique gold
- Santa, star and topiary stencils
- Stencil paint cremes: red, green, black, white, peach, goldenrod, brown
- Stencil adhesive
- Paintbrushes: No. 4 flat, sponge, six ¼" or ⅜" (6 mm or 1 cm) stencil
- Topcoat sealer spray
- Fruitwood gel wood stain
- Assorted trims: 4" (10 cm) square green plaid fabric, natural raffia, yellow waxed linen thread, 1½" x 2" (3.8 x 5 cm) wood star, 1½" (3.8 cm) square watercolor paper, green flat buttons: two ½" (1.3 cm) and one ¾" (2 cm)
- White craft glue
- Miscellaneous items: paint palette, paper towels, scissors, tracing paper, pencil, fine-point black permanent-ink marker

Step 3

1 *Basecoating:* Refer to the Painting Instructions and Techniques on page 160. Let paints and finishes dry between colors and coats. Use the sponge brush to basecoat the clock pale green. Use the No. 4 flat brush to paint the edges dark green.

2 *Stenciling Preparation:* Apply stencil adhesive to the back of the stencils and let dry until tacky. Refer to the photo to adhere the stencils to the clock, cutting the stencils to fit, if necessary. Remove the protective skin from each paint creme with a paper towel. Use a new stencil brush for each color. Fill the stencil brush with color and wipe the excess on a paper towel. Always start painting on the stencil itself and work into the open areas.

Step 6

3 *Stenciling:* Begin applying color in a circular motion holding the brush in a perpendicular position. Stencil Santa's beard and hat trim white, then shade lightly with black. See the Step 3 illustration to stencil the following: hat and topiary streamers with red, face with peach, stars with goldenrod, topiary pot with brown, topiary trunk with green.

4 *Staining:* Lightly spray the clock with sealer. Refer to the photo to lightly apply wood stain to the clock. Spray with another light mist of sealer.

5 *Stars:* Trace the star pattern to tracing paper, and cut out. Cut the star out from green plaid fabric, and refer to the photo to glue to the clock. Use 1 of the small star stencils to trace 1 star onto the watercolor paper, and cut out. Paint the paper star and the wood star antique gold. Glue the wood star to the clock, slightly overlapping the fabric star.

Step 7

6 *Details:* Refer to the the photo and use the black marker to draw "stitching" lines around the stars. See the Step 6 illustration to draw details and outlines around the Santa and topiary.

7 *Clock Hand Assembly:* Refer to the manufacturer's instructions to assemble the clock movement and to attach the clock hands. Glue the paper star to the clock's second hand, as shown in the Step 7 illustration.

8 *Button Trims:* Glue a ½" (1.3 cm) button to the topiary star. Cut an 8" (20.5 cm) length of waxed yellow linen thread and thread the ends through the holes in the other ½" (1.3 cm) button. Tie the ends in a bow and trim. Glue the button to the center of the wood star. Repeat to thread yellow thread through the holes in the ¾" (2 cm) button; knot, then cut the thread ends. Tie a raffia bow. Glue the bow and the ¾" (2 cm) button to the upper left top of the clock.

Star
Cut 1 from green plaid fabric
1 of 1

Primitive deer ornament

This little deer made of ultrasuede® is simple in design, and decorations—embroidery, buttons and pipe cleaners—finish the look. The ultrasuede is soft and smooth to the touch and gives a realistic feel to an animal ornament.

Materials

- Two 3" x 5" (7.5 x 12.5 cm) pieces brown or appropriate-colored Ultrasuede
- 3" (7.5 cm) of 6 mm tan chenille stem
- Scrap of polyester fiberfill
- Two ¼" to ⅜" (6 mm to 1 cm) buttons
- Black embroidery floss
- 8" (20.5 cm) thread or floss for hanging loop
- Miscellaneous items: tracing paper, pencil, straight pins, air-soluble marker, embroidery needle, scissors, transparent tape, sewing machine with matching or black thread, chopstick or knitting needle

1 *Pattern:* Trace the pattern to tracing paper, and cut out. Place pattern on the desired side of Ultrasuede, and trace around it onto the fabric with the air-soluble marker. Reverse the pattern, and place and trace on the other piece of Ultrasuede. Do not cut out the deer yet.

2 *Eyes:* Pin-mark the eye placement on each piece. Refer to the Embroidery Stitches on page 158 for how to make French knots. Use 2 strands of black embroidery floss to make double-wrap French knots for each eye.

3 *Antlers:* Cut chenille stem into three 1″ (2.5 cm) pieces. Tape the chenille stems onto the wrong side of 1 of the Ultrasuede pieces, as shown in the Step 3 illustration. Do not place tape where stitching will occur, 1/4″ (6 mm) from the edge.

Step 3

Desired side

Other side

4 *Assembly:* Place the Ultrasuede pieces together, right sides out, and pin. Machine- or hand-stitch 1/4″ (6 mm) in from the edges around the deer with short stitches, leaving a 1″ (2.5 cm) opening on the belly between the legs for stuffing. Stitch slowly over the pipe cleaners, taking care not to break the machine needle. Backstitch at the beginning and end of the stitching.

5 *Trimming:* Use the scissors to cut the fabric to a scant 1/8″ (3 mm) from the stitching; see the Step 5 illustration. Do not cut off the chenille stems, just the fabric around them. Do not trim the fabric at the opening yet.

Step 5

Opening for fiberfill. Do not trim.

6 *Stuffing:* Stuff the deer firmly with fiberfill. Stuff small pieces into the legs first, using a chopstick, knitting needle or small implement to reach into the ends. Then stuff tail and head, followed by the body. Hand-stitch the opening shut, matching the machine stitching. Trim the fabric around the opening area to a scant 1/8″ (3 mm) from the stitching.

7 *Finishing:* Trim and bend chenille stems for antler shape as desired. Sew buttons to back near center on front side with black embroidery floss. Thread floss or thread for hanging loop through a needle, and insert through the back near the buttons along the seamline. Check to see that the deer hangs evenly; adjust placement, if necessary. Remove needle, and tie thread or floss ends in an overhand knot.

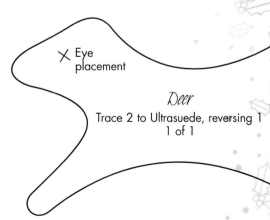

✕ Eye placement

Deer
Trace 2 to Ultrasuede, reversing 1
1 of 1

75

soldier Sock doll

This smiling soldier won't scare anybody off. With shiny brass buttons and a soft cuddly body made from socks, he's just dying to be hugged.

Materials

- Ladies size 9-11 ribbed-cuff cotton anklets: 1 each black, off-white; 2 red
- 9" x 12" (23 x 30.5 cm) black felt
- Paper-backed fusible web
- Polyester fiberfill
- Red embroidery floss
- 2 round black 6 mm beads
- 4 buttons, 3/8" (1 cm) gold round
- 1/3 yd. (0.32 m) black web belting, 1" (2.5 cm) wide
- 1" (2.5 cm) gold vest buckle
- Pattern Page 169
- Miscellaneous items: sewing needle, matching threads, tracing paper, pencil, scissors, air-soluble marker, ruler, sewing machine, iron

1 *Body:* Measure and cut 7" (18 cm) from toe of off-white sock; see the Step 1 illustration to save the cuff for the arms. Stuff foot of sock with fiberfill. Turn raw edges under 1/8" (3 mm) and slipstitch closed. Toe seam will be at back of head.

2 *Head:* Sew a running stitch around body 3" (7.5 cm) from top. Pull thread tight to form head; knot and trim. Refer to the photo and use air-soluble marker to mark eyes and mouth. Sew on black bead eyes. See the Embroidery Stitches on page 158 and use 2 strands of red floss to backstitch the mouth.

3 *Legs:* See the Step 1 illustration to cut ribbed cuff 6½" (16.3 cm) long from black sock. See the Step 3A illustration to cut cuff in half lengthwise. See 3B to fold each half lengthwise, right sides together, and machine-stitch 1/8" (3 mm) seam. Turn right side out; stuff each leg with fiberfill. Turn raw edges under 1/8" (3 mm) at top and slipstitch closed. Stitch across lower leg 1" (2.5 cm) from bottom for foot. Slipstitch legs to bottom of body.

4 *Jacket:* See the Step 1 illustration to cut ribbed cuff from 1 red sock and pull over body with finished edge at top. Roll down finished edge for collar. Turn under raw edges and sew to legs and lower body. Sew 4 buttons to jacket front. For belt, turn under 1 raw end of black webbing ½" (1.3 cm) and stitch. Insert opposite end of webbing through buckle and stitch to secure. Buckle belt around waist.

5 *Arms:* See the Step 1 illustration to measure and cut 5" (12.5 cm) from top of off-white cuff. Cut in half lengthwise and stitch arms the same as in the Step 3 illustration for legs. Turn right side out and stuff with fiberfill. Turn raw edges under at an angle so arms will hang at doll sides. To make each hand, sew a running stitch around arm 1" (2.5 cm) from end. Pull threads tight to form hand; knot and trim.

6 *Sleeves:* See the Step 1 illustration to cut 5" (12.5 cm) long cuff from remaining red sock. Cut as shown in the 3A illustration, and stitch as in 3B, except don't round the edge—make 2 long tubes, open at both ends. Turn right side out and pull over arm with finished edge at wrist, as shown in the Step 6 illustration. Turn under finished edge and slipstitch to wrist. Turn under raw edge at shoulder and stitch completed arm/sleeve to jacket.

7 *Hat:* Fuse web to black felt. Trace the patterns to tracing paper, and cut out. Trace the patterns onto the paper backing and cut from fused felt. Fit hat around head, with brim to the front, and stitch overlapping ends at back. Check the fit of hat top; trim as needed. Slipstitch to hat; insert a bit of fiberfill in hat and stitch to head.

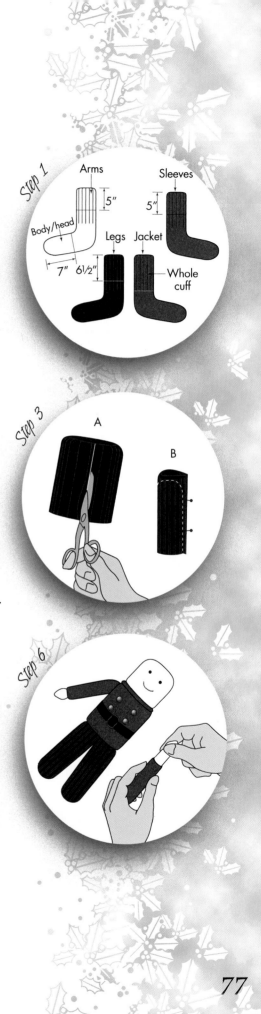

Woven pet coLLar

Your four-Legged friend can be struttin' in styLe wearing a one-of-a-kind coLLar with a woven floss accent handmade by a very proud owner.

Materials

- Embroidery floss, 1 skein each of 4 different colors
- Fabric pet collar
- Miscellaneous items: tape measure, scissors, safety pin or masking tape, sewing needle and thread to match collar

1 *Preparation:* Cut 2 strands of each floss color (A, B, C and D) 1¼ yd. (1.15 m) long. Arrange them in order as follows: A1 (first strand of A), B1, C1, D1, D2 (second strand of D), C2, B2, A2. Tie all 8 strands together in an overhand knot, leaving a 1" (2.5 cm) tail. Tape or pin the tail to a surface so the strands will be held in place while you work. Smooth the strands so they are in the right order.

2 *Row 1 First Knot:* See the Step 2A illustration to wrap A1 over, then under B1 to form a knot. Hold B1 firmly while pulling A1 toward the beginning overhand knot. Repeat to make a second small knot on top of the previous knot; see 2B. You have now completed a double knot around B1.

3 *Row 1 Left Side:* With A1, make a double knot around C1, then D1. Drop A1 at the center of the row, next to D1. See the Step 4 illustration.

4 *Row 1 Fourth Knot:* See the Step 4 illustration to make a knot at the far right side of the row by wrapping A2 over, then under B2. Hold B2 firmly while pulling A2 toward the beginning overhand knot. Repeat to make a second small knot on top of the previous knot to finish the double knot around B2.

5 *Row 1 Right Side:* With A2, make a double knot from the right around C2, D2 and A1 (which is now at the center of the row). The knots should slant diagonally from both sides toward the center as shown in the Step 5 illustration.

6 *Rows 2, 3, & 4:* At end of each row, the first strand on each side will be at the center. Knot as follows:
Row 2: With B1, make a double knot around C1, D1 and A2. With B2, make a double knot from the right around C2, D2, A1 and B1.
Row 3: With C1, make a double knot around D1, A2 and B2. With C2, make a double knot from the right around D2, A1, B1 and C1.
Row 4: With D1, make a double knot around A2, B2 and C2. With D2, make a double knot from the right around A1, B1, C1 and D1.

7 *Finishing:* You have now completed 1 color pattern. Repeat this color pattern until the floss collar is the desired length. Tie all the strands together in an overhand knot. Trim the tail to 1" (2.5 cm), the same length as the beginning tail. Place the floss collar on top of the fabric collar and hand-stitch down the center of the entire length with matching thread.

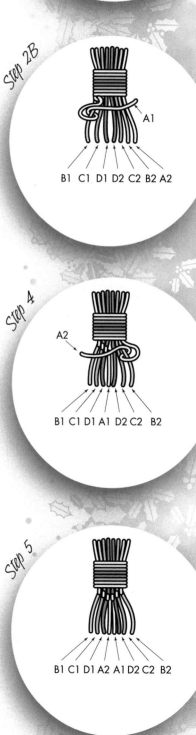

Step 2A

A1

B1 C1 D1 D2 C2 B2 A2

Step 2B

A1

B1 C1 D1 D2 C2 B2 A2

Step 4

A2

B1 C1 D1 A1 D2 C2 B2

Step 5

B1 C1 D1 A2 A1 D2 C2 B2

panel MANTEL topper

THIS INNOVATIVE MANTEL CLOTH WILL ADAPT TO ANY SIZE MANTEL. THE FRONT AND SIDE PANELS ARE STITCHED INDIVIDUALLY, AND THEN HELD IN PLACE ONTO THE TOP PIECE BY BRAIDED RIBBON KNOTTED BETWEEN BUTTONS.

Materials

- Red and gold decorator fabric, lining fabric, and lightweight batting—to determine actual yardage see Step 3
- Polyester fiberfill
- 5/8" (1.5 cm) gold buttons, 4 for each front and side panel
- Gold braid, 7 mm wide: 9" (23 cm) for each button; measure panel sides and bottom for yardage
- Weighted rod, 1" (2.5 cm) shorter than mantel width
- Assorted beads for tassel
- Pattern Sheet
- Miscellaneous items: tape measure, tracing or pattern paper, pencil, yardstick, scissors, rotary cutter and mat (optional), straight pins, sewing machine and matching threads, iron, sewing needle

1   *Measurements:* See the Step 1 illustration to measure the mantel. To get the front panel width, divide your mantel width by the number of front panels you want; 10" to 15" (25.5 to 38 cm) is a recommended width. The mantel in the photo is 51" (129.5 cm) wide. To have 4 front panels, each needs to be 12¾" (32.4 cm) wide. The panels are 13" (33 cm) long; the beaded tassels add another 3" (7.5 cm). All seam allowances are ½" (1.3 cm).

2   *Front Panel Pattern:* Cut a paper rectangle as shown in the Front Panel Pattern Guide on the Pattern Sheet. Fold the 15" (38 cm) ends together. Mark 1" (2.5 cm) from the bottom of 1 end along the fold, and 7" (18 cm) and 14" (35.5 cm) up from the bottom on each side. Draw dotted seamlines as shown, making the triangle point and top. Add on ½" (1.3 cm) outside the dotted seamlines, as shown. Make the End Panel pattern the same, except use a paper rectangle 1" (2.5 cm) wider than your mantel depth.

3   *Yardage:* See the Fabric Layout Guide on the Pattern Sheet to draw your pattern pieces on paper. 54" (137 cm) decorator fabric is assumed; adjust if you will use narrower or wider. Add ½" (1.3 cm) all around the mantel top. You will need the same amount of lining fabric and batting, plus an additional 4" (10 cm) strip of lining fabric for a rod pocket that will go the entire width of the mantel. Cut the end panels, front panels, rod pocket and mantel top from the decorator fabric, batting and lining fabric as drawn.

4   *Rod Pocket:* Fold ½" (1.3 cm) on the short ends, and stitch ¼" (6 mm) from the edge. Fold in half lengthwise, right side out, and press. Pin pocket, matching raw edges to outer edge as shown in the Step 4 illustration. Baste a scant ½" (1.3 cm) from the cut edges; edgestitch along the folded edge.

5   *Assembly:* Mark ½" (1.3 cm) seamline at all corners on the lining panels. Layer panel pieces as follows: batting, decorator fabric right side up, and lining marked and wrong side up. Pin and stitch around, leaving a 4" (10 cm) opening at the top. Trim batting seam allowances close to stitching and corners. Turn right side out, and press; slipstitch opening closed. Repeat to assemble the mantel top, making sure the lining piece is layered so the sleeve pocket will be on the outside. Hand-stitch gold braid to each panel sides and bottom; see photo.

6   *Buttons:* Sew 2 buttons to the top of each panel, ½" (1.3 cm) from the top and 2½" (6.5 cm) in from each side. Lay the mantel top and panels flat, as shown in the Step 6 illustration. Mark the corresponding button placement on the mantel top, and sew buttons on. Mark with tape as many gold braid pieces as buttons every 9" (23 cm); cut them apart in the center of the tape. Twist the braid, connecting 2 buttons in an S-shape. Tie the braid once, and bring the ends under and to the opposite sides. Make a square knot, leaving the second half loose to form a raised square knot. Tuck the ends underneath, and secure the knot with fabric glue.

7   *Tassels:* Use doubled thread and a sewing needle; knot the thread firmly at the end. Put a seed bead on first, catching the knot firmly in that bead; trim any thread ends. String desired beads until you have a tassel 3" (7.5 cm) long. Tack the beads to the end of a panel point; knot thread and cut. Repeat for all panel points. Insert weighted rod into rod pocket on the mantel top.

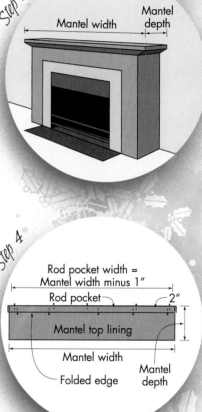

Step 1

Mantel width

Mantel depth

Step 4

Rod pocket width = Mantel width minus 1"

Rod pocket

2"

Mantel top lining

Mantel width

Folded edge

Mantel depth

Step 6

½"

2½"

ON dasher, on dancer

Materials

- Wood: 9" x 12" (23 x 30.5 cm) of 3/16" (4.5 mm) thickness for heads and feet, 8" x 9" (20.5 x 23 cm) of 1/8" (3 mm) thickness for muzzle hearts, 1 each eggs for bodies: 1 3/4" (4.5 cm), 2 1/2" (6.5 cm), 3 1/4" (8.2 cm), 4 1/4" (10.8 cm), 5" (12.5 cm)

- Wood sealer, satin acrylic spray
- Acrylic paints: dunes, black, rose, brown, bambi, putty, white, ivory

- Paintbrushes: 1/4" (6 mm) deerfoot stippler; Nos. 1 and 0 liner; Nos. 2, 4, 6, 8, and 10 flat
- 6" (15 cm) square lightweight canvas
- Red chenille stems: three 6 mm, two 9 mm
- Florals: six 12 mm green pine stems, 1 red berry pick, 5 mini silk holly leaves
- 3/8" (1 cm) jingle bells: 4 red, 2 gold
- Velvet craft ribbon: 1/3 yd. (0.32 m) green, 1/8" (3 mm) wide; 2/3 yd. (0.63 m) red, 1/8" (3 mm) wide; 1/4 yd. (0.25 m) green, 1/16" (1.5 mm) wide
- Tools: scroll saw, drill with 3/32" bit
- Glues: wood, hot glue gun
- Pattern Pages 174
- Miscellaneous items: tracing paper, pencil, fine sandpaper, tack cloth, brown paper bag, paint palette, synthetic sponge, transfer paper, stylus, scissors, wire cutters, ruler

Painted wood eggs and hearts make this cute, chubby reindeer family, who would be proud to pull santa's sleigh.

1 *Wood Preparation:* Refer to Painting Instructions and Techniques on page 160. Let paint and sealers dry between colors and coats. Use wood glue on wood pieces, and hot glue gun for decorations. Trace the patterns to tracing paper, and cut out. Trace the heads, muzzles and feet to wood, and cut out. Drill 4 holes as indicated on patterns on each head. Sand all surfaces with fine sandpaper, and remove dust with tack cloth. Brush on wood sealer with flat brush. Rub with brown paper bag to smooth.

Step 4

Glue on back side

2 *Basecoat:* Use flat brush to basecoat egg and head with dunes and feet with black. Mix bambi and ivory and lightly sponge egg; sponge again with bambi. Glue large end of egg to center of feet.

3 *Face:* Transfer face details, except hair, to head. Use liner brushes and black to paint eyes and lashes; highlight eyes with white. Shade eyebrows with brown and stipple lightly with putty. Use rose to shade cheeks and bottom edge of head for mouth; see the Step 4 illustration. Paint the hair strokes using liner brushes and bambi, dunes and brown. Highlight with putty.

Step 7

4 *Heart Muzzle:* Basecoat with dunes; shade each side of heart point with rose. Shade rounded bottom edges and paint 1 stroke halfway up center of muzzle with bambi. Paint black nose and highlight with white. Make brown dots on muzzle. Apply glue to back of muzzle and glue to head so shaded mouth shows at bottom; see the Step 4 illustration.

5 *Ears:* Basecoat canvas square front with dunes and back with bambi; trace 2 ears for each reindeer. On ear fronts, shade outside edges with bambi and float rose down center with darker color at base. Cut out ears just inside lines. Tightly roll both sides of each ear base to center. Glue in outermost holes facing forward.

Antler Cutting Guide

LENGTHS	WIDTH	# TO CUT
1" (2.5 cm)	6 mm	4
1½" (3.8 cm)	6 mm	6
1¾" (4.5 cm)	6 mm	6
2" (5 cm)	9 mm	4
2¼" (6 cm)	6 mm	2
2¼" (6 cm)	9 mm	4
2¾" (7 cm)	9 mm	2
3" (7.5 cm)	9 mm	2

6 *Assembly:* Paint furry chests on Nos. 3 and 5 with side-loaded strokes of dunes, bambi and brown highlighted with white. Refer to the photo to sand egg front where head will go. Glue head to body, tilting to 1 side. Spray all surfaces with acrylic spray; let dry.

7 *Antlers:* See the Antler Cutting Guide to cut chenille stems. See Assembly Guide and the Step 7 illustration to make antlers by wrapping prongs tightly once around stems, and bending. Glue a pair of antlers into remaining holes at top of each head.

Antler Assembly Guide

	2 STEM LENGTHS	4 PRONG LENGTHS
No. 1	1½" (3.8 cm)	1" (2.5 cm)
No. 2	1¾" (4.5 cm)	1½" (3.8 cm)
No. 3	2¼" (6 cm)	1¾" (4.5 cm)
No. 4	2¾" (7 cm)	2" (5 cm)
No. 5	3" (7.5 cm)	2¼" (6 cm)

8 *Decorating:* Use wire cutters to cut pine stems. Refer to the photo to hot-glue in clusters under chin of Nos. 1, 4 and 5. Glue 2 holly leaves under chin of No. 2 and 3 leaves on No. 3. Cut berry stems and glue in clusters on top of greenery on Nos. 1, 2 and 5. Glue jingle bells to greenery on No. 4. Refer to the photo to tie and glue bows on Nos. 2, 3, 4 and 5.

83

CHRISTMAS-
Sauruses

Have some prehistoric holiday fun with these whimsical christmas dinosaurs—a santa t-rex and gift-bearing Longneck stitched in perforated plastic.

Materials

- One sheet 14-count perforated plastic
- 1 skein each 6-strand embroidery floss in colors listed in Color Key
- No. 24 tapestry needle
- Two 4 mm wiggle eyes
- Miscellaneous items: scissors, white craft glue

1 *Preparation:* Refer to the Perforated Plastic/Paper General Instructions and Stitches on page 159 and the Stitch Charts. Follow the bold outlines to cut each design from perforated plastic. Each square on the graph represents a small square surrounded by 4 holes on the plastic. Symbols correspond to colors in the Color Key. Use 6 strands of floss for all stitches. Overcast all edges at same time with the same color. Refer to the photo to glue wiggle eyes on dinosaurs.

2 *Santa T-Rex:* Begin with the green mosaic stitches on the back. Fill in the rest of the body with green and medium green half cross-stitches. Complete the T-Rex with red and white cross-stitches on the hat.

3 *Longneck:* Begin with the green and red half cross-stitches on the present. Complete the rest of the body with dark and light purple diagonal Gobelin stitches. Finish the longneck with a French knot nostril and backstitched mouth in dark purple.

Santa T-Rex Stitch Chart

Longneck Stitch Chart

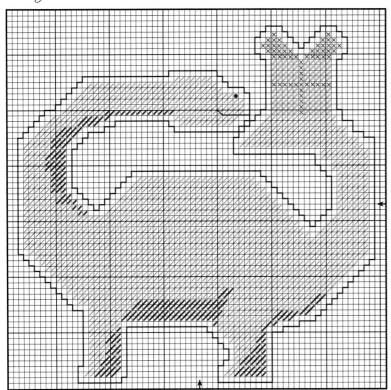

Santa T-Rex Color Key

SYMBOL	COLOR
o	White Cross Stitch
×	Red Cross Stitch
/	Green Half Cross
◢	Med. Green Half Cross
◿	Green Mosaic

Longneck Color Key

SYMBOL	COLOR
◿	Dk. Green Half Cross
×	Red Half Cross
/	Lt. Purple Diagonal Gobelin
◢	Dk. Purple Diagonal Gobelin
●	Dk. Purple French Knot
—	Dk. Purple Backstitches

Cinnamon stick
wall hanging

Fuse and embroider a simple design on muslin and display it in a primitive frame cleverly constructed from cinnamon sticks.

(embroidered sampler reads:)

Grandma's Gingerbread

Cream 1 c. each:
soft oleo, brown sugar
Add 1 c. molasses
and 3 eggs
Sift together
4 c. flour
1 t. ginger, 1 t. salt,
1 t. baking powder

Mix dry ingredients
with molasses mixture
Roll on lightly floured
surface and cut with
cookie cutters
Bake on lightly greased
cookie sheet at 350°

Materials

- Four ¾" (2 cm) diameter cinnamon sticks, 12" (30.5 cm) long
- 16" (40.5 cm) jute twine
- Fabrics: 9" x 12" (23 x 30.5 cm) unbleached muslin, 4" (10 cm) square golden brown brushed denim, three 2" (5 cm) squares coordinating small prints
- Fusible web
- Embroidery floss: green, tan
- Four ¾" (2 cm) flat dark red buttons
- 9" x 14" (23 x 35.5 cm) quilt batting
- Pattern Sheet
- Miscellaneous items: craft knife, ruler, scissors, hot glue gun, tracing paper, fine-line black permanent-ink marker, pencil, iron, 9" x 14" (23 x 35.5 cm) lightweight matboard or cardboard, embroidery needle, masking tape, craft wire, wire cutters

1 *Frame:* Use the craft knife to cut 2 cinnamon sticks to 9" (23 cm). Refer to the photo to position the 12" (30.5 cm) sticks on top of the shorter sticks at right angles, creating an approximately 6½" x 8½" (16.3 x 21.8 cm) frame opening. Tie the sticks together at the corners with jute twine, knotting the twine at the back. Spot-glue the sticks on the back to secure.

2 *Patterns:* Trace the 4 small patterns to tracing paper and cut them out. Use the black marker to trace the recipe onto tracing paper. Center the traced recipe under the muslin and use the marker to trace the recipe onto the muslin.

3 *Appliqués:* Refer to the manufacturer's instructions to fuse the web to the wrong side of the brushed denim and print fabrics. Trace the 4 small patterns onto the paper backing of the appropriate fused fabrics, and cut them out. Refer to the pattern and the Step 3 illustration to fuse the gingerbread man, hearts and the star onto the muslin. Use the marker to draw the eyes on the gingerbread man and the stitching lines around each appliqué.

4 *Embroidery:* Sew the 4 buttons to the muslin with tan embroidery floss. Use the tan floss to embroider 3 X's for buttons down the center front of the gingerbread man. See Embroidery Stitches on page 158 to backstitch the stems around the flower buttons with green floss.

5 *Mounting:* Cut the quilt batting and the lightweight cardboard each into two 7" x 9" (18 x 23 cm) pieces. Layer: the muslin, right side down, both batting pieces and 1 cardboard rectangle on top. Pull the edges of the muslin onto the back of the cardboard, stretching the design taut and mitering the corners. Use masking tape to secure, as shown in the Step 5 illustration. Center and glue the remaining cardboard rectangle over the taped back.

6 *Assembly:* Place the mounted design on the frame from the back, and trim any edges, if necessary. Spot-glue the design along the edges to secure. To make a hanger, thread 1 end of craft wire through the jute at a top back corner. Twist the wire end to secure. Cut the wire a little longer than the frame width; see the Step 6 illustration. Thread and secure the wire end same as for the other end.

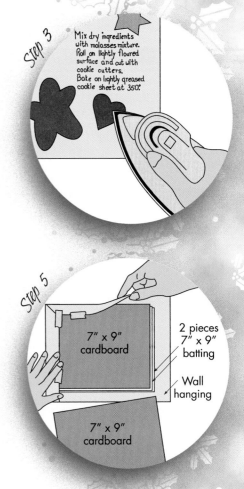

Step 3

Mix dry ingredients with molasses mixture. Roll on lightly floured surface and cut with cookie cutters. Bake on lightly greased cookie sheet at 350°.

Step 5

7" x 9" cardboard

2 pieces 7" x 9" batting

Wall hanging

7" x 9" cardboard

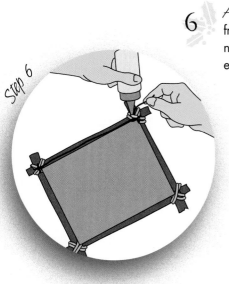

Step 6

gingerbread tin topper

Materials

- 39-bar square 7-mesh plastic canvas
- Plastic canvas yarn: 18 yd. (16.56 m) black; 5 yd. (4.6 m) brown; 2 yd. (1.85 m) each green, pink, red
- No. 16 tapestry needle
- 20" (51 cm) ivory ruffled lace, 3/4" (2 cm) wide
- 7" (18 cm) or larger cookie tin
- White craft glue
- Pattern Page 166

Glued onto the lid, a stitched gingerbread will be enjoyed long after the home-baked goodies are gone!

1 *Preparation:* Refer to the Plastic Canvas Instructions and Stitches on page 159. Follow Stitch Chart on page 166 to cut the design. Cut up to, but not into, the edge bars. Each line on the chart represents 1 bar of plastic canvas.

2 *Stitching:* Cross-stitch the eyes, nose, cheeks, hearts and holly berries. Work remainder of the design with continental stitches, filling in the background with black. Backstitch the mouth with black, and the holly leaves with holly green, stitching over continental background. Overcast edges with black.

3 *Finishing:* Glue lace around edges on back, overlapping start at bottom of design. Glue stitched piece to tin lid.

it's in THE BAG

WRAP UP YOUR gift wrap
WORRIES WITH simple-to-sew gift bags.

Materials

- 15" x 18" (38 x 46 cm) fabric
- 1 yd. (0.95 m) coordinating ribbon or cord
- Miscellaneous items: scissors, sewing machine and matching thread, iron

1 With right sides together, stitch 1/2" (1.3 cm) seam along 15" (38 cm) length. Press seam open.

2 Fold top edge down 1/4" (6 mm) and press. Turn under another 3" (7.5 cm) and sew hem. The deep hem allows for a nicely finished look once the bag is tied.

3 Fold fabric tube with seam down center back of bag. Pin along bottom of bag, as shown in the Step 3 illustration. Stitch 1/2" (1.3 cm) seam, trim corners, turn and press. Fill the bag with gift and tie with ribbon or cord.

Step 3

8 1/2"

3"

11 3/4"

fabulous fabric frame

a frame covered with silky satin makes a great christmas gift, if you can bear to part with it!

Materials

- Wood picture frame
- Fusible knit interfacing and gold lightweight slippery fabric. Measure the outside length and width of the frame, and add on 2" (5 cm) all around; you will need a piece of fabric and interfacing twice that size.
- Adhesives: spray mount, permanent fabric, jewelry

- Embellishments: sequins, seed beads, ribbon. Measure inner frame opening for ribbon yardage, and have a width no greater than the space between the glass and the edge of the frame.
- Miscellaneous items: fine sandpaper, tape measure, ruler, tracing or pattern paper, pencil, scissors, straight pins, fabric marker, round toothpicks

1 *Preparation:* Remove frame back and glass from the frame. Lightly sand the frame surface to remove finish. When using spray adhesive, spray in an area away from your work area, and cover the surface to protect from overspray.

2 *Measuring:* See the Step 2 illustration to measure; use the tape and take a continuous measurement in both directions. Add 2″ (5 cm) to each of those measurements; cut a rectangle of fusible interfacing slightly larger than the measurement. Follow the manufacturer's instructions to fuse to the wrong side of the lightweight fabric.

3 *Frame Covering:* Use the fabric marker to draw a rectangle with the Step 2 measurement on the fused side; cut out for frame covering.

4 *Frame Backing:* Place the frame on the remaining fabric and use the fabric marker to trace around the outside edge of the frame and the inner opening. Cut out this piece for the frame backing about 1/8″ to 1/4″ (3 to 6 mm) narrower on both edges.

5 *Frame Opening:* Place the frame covering fused side up on a flat work surface. Place the frame wrong side up on the fabric. Use the fabric marker to trace around the inside of the frame opening. Pick up the frame and measure the frame-opening depth. See the Step 5 illustration to draw another rectangle inside that is the frame-opening depth away. Draw diagonal lines at the corners. Cut out the smallest rectangle; clip the corners at the marked diagonal lines, stopping just short of the corners.

6 *Adhering:* Place frame covering fused side up; apply spray adhesive. Place on a flat work surface, fused and sprayed side up. Place the frame on the fabric, wrong side up, centering the frame opening over the cut-out opening. Press it on, and gently bring the fabric up around the frame edges and sides.

7 *Outer Edges:* Clip fabric diagonally at the outside corners, stopping short of the frame front edge. Smooth the fabric around corners at the opposite ends. Tuck under fabric on the adjoining side to form a smooth covered corner; trim excess fabric. Apply fabric adhesive with a toothpick in any loose spots to secure tightly.

8 *Finishing:* Apply spray adhesive to the frame backing, fused side up. Center it on the frame back, and smooth down. Apply spray adhesive to ribbon, and glue around the inner opening to cover the bare wood at the corners. Butt the ends together. Apply jewelry adhesive with a toothpick to the back of sequins and beads, and embellish the frame front as desired.

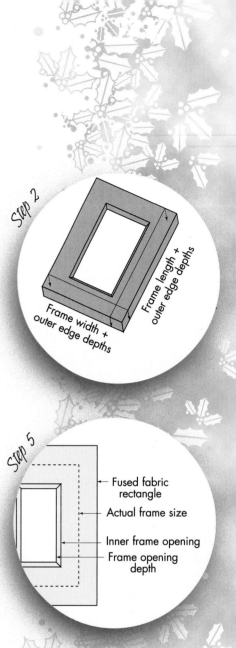

Step 2

Frame length + outer edge depths

Frame width + outer edge depths

Step 5

Fused fabric rectangle
Actual frame size
Inner frame opening
Frame opening depth

Pot Belly
pals

these hollow shapes have back cutouts so they can hold cookies, candy, or even a surprise present, or hang from a knob or hook.

Materials

FOR SANTA OR RUDOLPH

- Papier mâché pot belly shape
- Acrylic paints: *for both:* white, black, red, green; *for Santa only:* stoneware blue, clay, apricot; *for Rudolph only:* mustard, antique white
- Paintbrushes: Nos. 2, 6 and 12 flat; fine liner; used coarse bristle; 1" (2.5 cm) sponge
- ½ yd. (0.5 m) green wired paper twist, Christmas floral pick
- Waterbase varnish, clear matte acrylic spray finish
- Pattern Sheet

FOR SANTA ONLY

- Trims: 2" (5 cm) white pom-pom, 1 yd. (0.95 m) Christmas plaid ribbon, 1" (2.5 cm) wide

FOR RUDOLPH ONLY

- 1½" (3.8 cm) wood ball knob
- 9" x 12" (23 x 30.5 cm) 140-lb. (63 kg) watercolor paper
- 6" (15 cm) square canvas
- Natural raffia
- Miscellaneous items: craft knife, ruler, scissors, glue gun, thick white craft glue, pencil, awl, paint palette, tracing and graphite paper, stylus, paper towels

1. *Preparation:* Remove stem from pot belly. Cut away any excess material around the hole. For Rudolph, unfold the stem; cut a 1" (2.5 cm) square piece. Use craft glue to glue the paper over hole. Use the sponge brush to seal pot belly with waterbase varnish.

2. *Painting:* Refer to the Painting Instructions and Techniques on page 160. Let paints and finishes dry between colors and coats. Paint as many coats as necessary for complete coverage. Use the appropriate size flat paintbrush, unless otherwise indicated.

3. *Santa Opening:* See the Step 3A illustration to determine pot belly front and back. Lightly pencil-mark an opening on the back side; use the craft knife to cut out. Poke holes for the handle in the sides, as shown in 3B. Use the sponge brush to paint the inside with green.

4. *Santa Face:* Trace the Santa pattern onto tracing paper. Place the pattern on the pot belly front. Use graphite paper and stylus to transfer only the beard, mustache, mouth and hat fur. Continue hat fur outline all around the back. Basecoat the face with apricot. Sideload with clay and shade outer edges. Transfer the face detail lines. Use the liner brush to paint the eyes, lashes and mouth black. Mix red and apricot, and shade cheek. Mix clay and apricot, sideload brush, and paint the nose.

Santa Hair & Fur: Basecoat the beard, mustache, eyebrows and hat fur with blue. Paint the lips and the rest of pot belly with red. Overstroke the mustache and eyebrows with white, but don't completely cover the blue. Use the coarse-bristle brush to dry-brush the hat fur and beard with white; see the Step 5 illustration.

Finishing Santa: Insert paper twist ends in holes, bend ends up and glue. Lightly spray Santa, inside and out, with at least 2 coats of acrylic finish. Make a multi-loop bow and tie to handle. Hot-glue floral pick to bow. Hot-glue pom-pom to center top of head.

Rudolph Patterns: See the Step 7 illustration and repeat Step 3, also cutting 1½" (3.8 cm) antler slits. Mark ear and nose placement. Trace the 4 Rudolph patterns to tracing paper, and cut out. Cut out the antlers and ears as indicated on the patterns. Use the sponge brush to basecoat the pot belly and canvas ears with mustard. Basecoat the paper antlers with antique white. Use the No. 12 flat brush, sideload with mustard and shade the antler edges. Paint the wood ball nose with red.

Rudolph Face: Refer to the Step 7 illustration, and use graphite paper and stylus to transfer the eye and mouth patterns. Basecoat the eyes white. Use the liner brush to paint green irises with white comma stroke highlights. Add a white dot in each eye and pull from the center to paint a star highlight. Outline the eyes and make mouth with black and the liner brush. Mix white with red to make pink, and float on cheeks.

Finishing Rudolph: Slit ears with craft knife as marked on the pattern. Overlap sections, cupping ears forward, and glue together. Refer to the Step 7 illustration to glue ears to head. Insert antler ends ¾" (2 cm) into slits. Inside head, bend ends back and glue. Glue the nose above the mouth. Repeat Step 6 to finish, except for pom-pom.

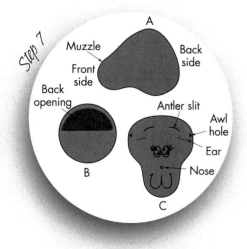

93

Nutcracker
sweet

Our nutcracker, designed for an intermediate painter, is painted with fabric dyes, then highlighted with a pearlizer. metallic scrolls and dots add a finishing touch to this delightful holiday design.

Materials

- Cotton-blend black knit shirt
- Fabric dyes: ruby, coral, topaz, malachite, sapphire, pink, onyx, mabe pearl, pearlizer
- Dimensional fabric glitter paint: glitzy blue, glitzy gold
- Fabric paintbrushes: Nos. 4, 6, 8 flat; No. 6 scrubber; No. 2/0 liner

- Trims: 36 iridescent oval pearl 3 x 6 mm beads, 12 round red ⅝" (1.5 cm) buttons, gold shoulder cord, ½" (1.3 cm) button, and 4" (10 cm) black twill tape
- ½ yd. (0.5 m) tulle
- Posterboard, ⅞" x 15" (2.2 x 38 cm) strip
- Pattern Sheet
- Miscellaneous items: tape measure, masking tape, T-shirt board, fine-point permanent-ink marker, chalk pencil, paint palette, paper towels, straight pin, sewing needle, matching threads

1 *Preparation & Pattern:* Wash and dry shirt; do not use fabric softener. Measure shirt front and mark center and a line from neck to shirt bottom with chalk pencil. Insert T-shirt board and secure with masking tape. Use the black marker to trace the pattern onto the tulle. Center pattern on shirt front with top of hat 3½" (9 cm) below neck seam, and pin. Draw over main pattern lines with chalk pencil to transfer to shirt, as seen in the Step 1 illustration.

2 *Undercoat:* Refer to the Painting Instructions and Techniques on page 160. Let paints dry between colors and coats. Use the appropriate size flat brush for all painting, and the liner for details. Use the No. 6 scrubber to undercoat-paint the Nutcracker and holly leaves 1 section at a time with mabe pearl, except for the hat brim.

3 *Body:* Paint hat and trousers sapphire. Highlight center of legs and hat with mabe pearl; repeat. Load brush with sapphire and side-load with pearlizer; apply lightly to trousers and hat to add shimmer. Paint the jacket pink, side-loading brush with mabe pearl; repeat. Basecoat the boots with a mixture of mabe pearl and onyx. Paint the boot laces and add highlights with mabe pearl.

4 *Leaves:* Load brush with malachite and sapphire and paint some holly leaves; paint remaining leaves malachite and topaz. Brush leaves lightly with pearlizer. Use onyx to paint the main leaf line, and onyx or glitzy gold randomly for the remaining lines.

5 *Details:* Use the tulle pattern and chalk to transfer the hat, boot and clothing details, or paint them freehand. Use glitzy gold to paint the belt, cuffs, epaulets, collar, hat brim and jacket trim. Refer to the Step 5 illustration; apply a second coat. Use the black marker to draw or the onyx to paint decorative lines on hat, belt, jacket, sleeves and boots.

6 *Hands, Face & Hair:* Double-load the No. 4 flat brush with coral and topaz and paint the hands and face with topaz toward the outside; repeat. Transfer face details. Blend coral with a dot of ruby and paint cheeks. Paint the mouth ruby, outline the nose and eyes, and paint pupils black. Add mabe pearl eye highlights. Paint beard, hair and mustache with mabe pearl and onyx strokes; add onyx accent lines.

7 *Curlicues & Dots:* Follow dimensional paint manufacturer's suggestions to use and dry, shaking paint thoroughly and holding close to but not touching fabric. Squeeze gently, wipe nozzle often; pop air bubbles immediately with pin. Referring to the photo, make the gold and blue curlicues around Nutcracker and leaves. Mark 1" (2.5 cm) increments along both edges of posterboard strip. See the Step 7 illustration to use strip as a guide to make gold dots.

8 *Finishing:* Refer to the photo and use matching threads to sew on oval beads and red buttons for holly berries. Slipstitch twill tape to wrong side of the shirt on the left shoulder seam, beginning at neck seam. Sew button on outside of the shirt on the shoulder seam at end of twill tape. Loop gold shoulder cord over button.

Step 1

Step 5

Step 7

Lace tree skirt

a simple lace circle with an underlayment of glistening gold lends an aura of quiet elegance to any christmas tree. and nothing could be easier to make than this— no sewing, only cutting and gluing!

Materials

- Lace tree skirt panel, available in various sizes, colors and designs. Featured in the photo is a 48" (122 cm) diameter circle.
- Gold lamé, or other desired fabric, in an amount to fit under lace tree skirt

- 4¼ yd. (3.9 m) red/gold braid for outer edge only of 48" (122 cm) tree skirt. See Step 4 for figuring yardage for your tree skirt.
- Fabric glue
- Seam sealer
- Miscellaneous items: scissors, straight pins

1   *Cutting Tree Skirt:* Place the lace tree skirt panel on a hard, flat work surface. Smooth out all wrinkles. Use scissors to trim off the outside edge of the lace to form a circle. Cut out the opening in the center of the tree skirt, making it slightly larger than your tree trunk, if that size is known.

2   *Cutting Underlayment:* Remove the tree skirt, and lay the gold lamé on the work surface. Place the tree skirt over the lamé, and loosely pin from the center outward to hold fabrics together. Because the lace design has a lot of give to it, the tree skirt will not be a perfect circle. Using the lace tree skirt as the pattern for cutting the underlayment of gold lamé will ensure that the 2 pieces will match. Cut the gold lamé as shown in the Step 2 illustration. Apply seam sealer to cut outer edge of gold lamé, leaving the 2 layers pinned.

3   *Back Opening:* If you use an everlasting tree, you can put the underlayment and lace tree skirt over the tree trunk, as it is being assembled. If you use a fresh tree, you will need to cut a back opening in the underlayment and tree skirt layers. Pin-mark a line using a yardstick, and cut through both layers as shown in the Step 3 illustration. Apply seam sealer to the back opening edges of gold lamé.

4   *Calculating Trim Yardage:* Multiply the diameter of your tree skirt by pi or 3.14. For the example in the photo multiply the 48" (122 cm) diameter by 3.14 for 151" (385.5 cm) or 4.2 yd. (3.86 m). If you have cut a back opening, you will need to use a tape measure to measure those edges, and the inner opening too.

5   *Trim:* Apply seam sealer to the beginning braid end, and to the final end, when cut. For a tree skirt for an everlasting tree, use fabric glue to apply decorative braid to outer edge only of the lace tree skirt. For a tree skirt for a fresh tree, see the Step 5 illustration, and begin and end the braid on the inner opening edges.

97

father Christmas

Re-create the twinkling eyes and bushy beard of father christmas with this victorian santa sewn with muslin and prequilted fabric. he will bring the spirit of giving to your home for the holiday season.

Materials

- 45" (115 cm) fabrics: ½ yd. (0.5 m) each; muslin, quilted reversible red/green, red plaid cotton/blend; 9" x 14" (23 x 35.5 cm) brown tweed

- 2 yd. (1.85 m) red/white stripe bias binding

- 1 package double-fold bias tape to match coat lining

- 1 yd. (0.95 m) brown cording

- 24-oz. (750 g) bag polyester fiberfill

- 2-lb. (1 kg) bag plastic filler beads

- 5 yd. (4.6 m) off-white coarse wool yarn or roving

- Two ³⁄₁₆" (4.5 mm) black beads

- Decorations: 12" (30.5 cm) pine tree with tiny pinecones and berry sprigs, 4½" (11.5 cm) teddy bear, candy canes to fill bag

- Pattern Sheet

- Miscellaneous items: tracing paper, pencil, scissors, water-soluble marker, straight pins, matching threads, sewing machine, sewing needle, black fine-point permanent-ink marker, pink powdered blush, hot glue gun

1 *Patterns:* Trace the patterns onto tracing paper, and cut out as indicated. Transfer markings with soluble marker. Also cut: from quilted fabric, two 5" x 10" (12.5 x 25.5 cm) pieces for sleeves and one 5¾" x 13" (14.5 x 33 cm) piece for hood; 15" x 21" (38 x 53.5 cm) of muslin for body and 16" x 30" (40.5 x 76 cm) of plaid fabric for underdress. Stitch all seams right sides together with ¼" (6 mm) seams; clip curves and turn right side out.

2 *Body:* Stitch 15" (38 cm) sides together for back seam. Pin to the base; stitch together. Pour filler beads into body; stuff firmly with fiberfill to finish. Sew a gathering stitch around the top, pull tightly and stitch shut.

3 *Arms:* Stitch 2 arm pieces together, lightly stuff hand with fiberfill. Topstitch fingers, and finish stuffing arm. Align X's by pinching arm, and tack to make elbow; see the Step 3 illustration. Bend left elbow and glue to hold. Turn top raw edges to inside, and whipstitch to body 5" (12.5 cm) from back seam.

Step 3

Body

4 *Head:* Stitch center front seam, stopping at the large dot. Match notches and dots, and stitch back to front. Use fiberfill to firmly stuff head; slipstitch bottom closed. Sew black bead eyes; draw eyebrows and mouth with black marker. Color cheeks and lips with blush. Pinch A's and B's together and tack loosely for the nose.

5 *Hair & Beard:* Cut yarn into 11" (28 cm) lengths. Separate 5 lengths into strands and fold in half. Stitch strands along the fold to the beard placement line. For the mustache, cut 2 lengths into 3" (7.5 cm) pieces and tack between the nose and mouth. See the Step 5 illustration. For the hair, separate the remaining yarn into individual strands and fold in half. Sandwich yarn between 2 small pieces of paper, machine-stitch through the center several times and tear away paper. Hot-glue hair to head.

Step 5

6 *Underdress:* Place 16" (40.5 cm) sides together, match plaids and stitch an 11" (28 cm) seam, leaving 5" (12.5 cm) open for armhole. Cut a 5" (12.5 cm) slit from top for second armhole on opposite side. Turn raw edges to inside, and hem. Topstitch ¼" (6 mm) around bottom edge. Sew a gathering stitch around the top and place underdress on body. Pull gathers tightly and knot. Hot-glue head to top of body.

7 *Coat:* Stitch back and fronts together at shoulder seams. Pin and stitch in 10" (25.5 cm) edges of sleeves, matching at sleeve placement marks. Stitch side seams together, beginning at bottom and ending at sleeve hems. Fold hood piece, right sides together, matching 5¾" (14.5 cm) edges. Stitch hood piece together along 6½" (16.3 cm) edge. Match hood seam and coat center back, and pin hood to coat neck as shown in the Step 7 illustration, matching hood edges at hood placement marks. Stitch; bind hood and neck seams with double-face tape. Stitch; bind hood, coat front edges and hem and sleeves with striped binding. Place coat on Father Christmas and turn back cuffs and front hood.

Step 7

8 *Bag:* Stitch side and bottom edges. Turn under casing at foldline, and stitch. Cut cord opening in casing, thread cord through and tie a knot in each end. Hot-glue right hand closed over cords. Fill bag with candy canes and teddy bear. Place tree in left arm and hot-glue hand around tree trunk.

Old-time wooden
ornaments

these ornaments hark back to simpler times, with tin soldiers under the tree, and colored glass balls decorating the branches.

Materials

FOR WOOD SOLDIER
- 1¼" (3.2 cm) wooden candle cup and ball
- Acrylic paints: red, peach, black, gold
- Paintbrushes: ½" (1.3 cm) flat, liner
- Satin finish waterbase varnish
- Trims: 4" (10 cm) white/gold edge satin ribbon, ⅛" (3 mm) wide; ¼ yd. (0.25 m) gold cord for hanger; ½" (1.3 cm) white/gold pom-pom
- Miscellaneous items: paint palette, paper towels, scissors, hot glue gun

Step 3 – Wood Soldier

Wood Soldier

1 *Preparation:* Refer to Painting Instructions and Techniques on page 160. Let paint dry between coats and colors. Use the flat brush to basecoat the ball with peach and the candle cup with red; use 2 coats if necessary for complete coverage. Paint candle cup rim gold for hat brim. Refer to the photo to paint gold comma strokes on hat front with liner brush.

2 *Face:* Refer to the photo. Dot eyes black and nose and mouth red. Dry-brush red cheeks. Use liner brush to paint black mustache. Brush a light coat of satin varnish on head and hat.

3 *Finishing:* Refer to the photo and the Step 3 illustration to hot-glue ribbon around head, beginning on top. Hot-glue hat to cover ribbon ends. Knot ends of gold cord to make hanger loop and hot-glue knot to top of hat. Hot-glue pom-pom to cover knot.

Materials

FOR 1 FROSTY BALL

- 1½" x ⅛" (3.8 cm x 3 mm) round wood disc
- Paints: metallic acrylic paints: green, aquamarine, sapphire, amethyst, red; textured snow paint; clear iridescent glitter paint
- Paintbrushes: 1" (2.5 cm) sponge; used small stiff bristle
- Acrylic matte spray finish
- 20-gauge copper wire, 1¼" (3.2 cm)
- Fast-drying clear adhesive
- 6" (15 cm) ribbon or cord, ⅛" (3 mm) wide
- White opaque paint marker (optional)
- Miscellaneous items: paint palette, wax paper, hot glue gun, wire cutters, needlenose pliers, pencil

Frosty Ball

1   *Painting:* Cover work surface with wax paper. Paint 1 side and edge of disc with metallic paint. Let paints dry between colors and coats.

2   *Snow:* Refer to the photo and the Step 2 illustration and use stiff brush to dab textured paint on upper disc and edges to resemble snow. Apply a thin coat of glitter paint over snow. Spray with matte finish.

3   *Finishing:* Bend wire in half over dowel or pencil to make a loop. Use adhesive to glue wire ends to upper disc back so that loop extends above top. Write name in center disc front with marker. Tie ribbon or cord through loop and hang on Christmas tree or tie to package as a gift tag.

Step 2 – Frosty Ball

THE GREAT OUTDOORS

What would winter be without snow? Wherever you live, conjure up a white Christmas and bring the outdoors inside with a few natural creations.

BuiLd me a SNOWMAN

You won't even need your mittens when you build this snowman by painting, stenciling and stacking papier mâché boxes.

Materials

- Papier mâché boxes, one each: 6½" (16.3 cm), 7¾" (19.9 cm), 9¼" (23.6 cm), 10¼" (26.1 cm)
- Wooden shapes: 2¼" (6 cm) tree, ¾" (2 cm) star, 1¼" (3.2 cm) knob, five 1" (2.5 cm) buttons
- Acrylic paints: mauve, green, blue, white, ivory, beige, yellow ochre
- Paintbrushes: ⅜" (1 cm) and 1" (2.5 cm) flat, Nos. 1 and 4 liner, ⅜" (1 cm) angle, sea sponge, small sponge pouncer, old toothbrush
- All-purpose primer, satin varnish
- Dimensional paste and a 3" (7.5 cm) star mold or three 3" (7.5 cm) wooden stars, ⅛" (3 mm) thick
- Stencils: ⅜" and ⅞" (1 and 2.2 cm) checks, ⅜" (1 cm) dots and spray stencil adhesive
- Pattern Page 165
- Miscellaneous items: sandpaper, tack cloth, paint palette, metal ruler, tape measure, low-tack tape, tracing paper, pencils, stylus, graphite paper, sea wool sponge, paper towels, thick white craft glue, black fine-point permanent-ink marker

1 *Preparation:* Mix equal parts primer and water and use flat brush to apply to all wood and boxes. Let dry between coats and colors. Sand lightly and remove dust with the tack cloth. Refer to Painting Instructions and Techniques on page 160 and the photo throughout. Use the 1" (2.5 cm) flat brush for basecoating. When using liner brushes, thin the paint to an ink-like consistency. Use the pouncer to stencil, and stencil adhesive to hold on stencils.

2 *Embellishments:* Mix a dot of yellow with ½ cup (125 mL) dimensional paste. Follow the manufacturer's instructions to make 3 stars with the mold, or use wooden stars. Paint 2 buttons mauve, 3 buttons blue, wooden stars yellow and the knob and tree green. Draw marker stitch lines along the star edges.

3 *Top Box:* Basecoat the 6½" (16.3 cm) box and lid top with blue and the lid rim with beige. Use the small flat brush to paint yellow stripes on box and rim. Use the No. 1 liner to paint narrow blue and ivory stripes on the rim, as shown in the Step 3 illustration. Mix blue and ivory and paint lt. blue and wavy beige lines on the box.

4 *Second Box:* Use the sea sponge and ivory to sponge-paint the box sides; randomly sponge over the ivory with beige. Stencil white dots on the box sides. Trace the pattern to tracing paper, and cut out; transfer the face to the box. Mix yellow and mauve to make orange; use the angle brush to paint the nose. Shade the bottom of the nose with mauve. Mix ivory, mauve and a little water to paint the cheeks with the angle brush. Use mauve and the No. 1 liner to paint cross-hatch lines on the cheeks; use the No. 4 liner to paint the mouth. Use the marker to draw the eyes, eyebrows, the open mouth and to outline the nose and cheeks; see the Step 4 illustration. Use the No. 1 liner to paint ivory highlights on the cheeks and eyes.

5 *Second & Third Box Lids:* Basecoat 7¾" (19.9 cm) lid with blue; stencil small yellow checks around the rim. Basecoat the 9¼" (23.6 cm) lid with green. Use the ruler to lightly pencil a 1¼" (3.2 cm) diamond grid on the top and rim. Use the No. 1 liner and ivory to paint the lines by placing the ruler a short distance from each penciled line and resting your little finger on the ruler; pull the brush toward you. Paint a mauve dot in the center of each diamond.

6 *Third & Bottom Boxes:* Stack the Second, Third and Bottom boxes on top of each other. Refer to the photo and the Step 6 illustration to pencil in the vest lines on the Third Box. Mask off the Bottom Box bottom border. Draw a curved line on the Bottom Box lid and lid side, and down to the border. Follow Step 4 to sponge-paint and stencil white dots on the vest. Basecoat rest of the body mauve; stencil large beige checks. Mask off a ¼" (6 mm) border around the Bottom Box bottom and paint it blue. Make yellow dots in the center of the mauve checks on the Bottom Box only. Use the No. 4 liner to paint wavy ivory and green lines.

7 *Finishing:* Glue 1 star centered on top of Top Box lid, then 2 mauve buttons and the knob. Glue remaining stars to Third Box; dot 2 mauve buttonholes in the center of each with the No. 4 liner. Use the marker to draw a line connecting the stars. Glue 3 blue buttons to Third and Bottom Boxes. Sand the tree and star edges; glue 2" (5 cm) from the bottom button. Spatter all boxes and lids by loading the toothbrush with thinned white paint and pulling your thumb over the bristles. Use the flat brush to apply 2 coats of satin varnish all over.

HOLLY
Napkin Rings

Make mealtimes especially festive during the holidays with these quick and easy napkin rings. But ring out the old look made with felt, and bring on the new—make them with ultrasuede®.

Materials

FOR EACH NAPKIN RING

- 4½" x 10" (11.5 x 25.5 cm) green Ultrasuede
- Three ¼" to ⅜" (6 mm to 1 cm) red wood beads
- 18" (46 cm) square napkin
- Miscellaneous items: tracing paper, pen, scissors, craft knife, sewing needle, red thread

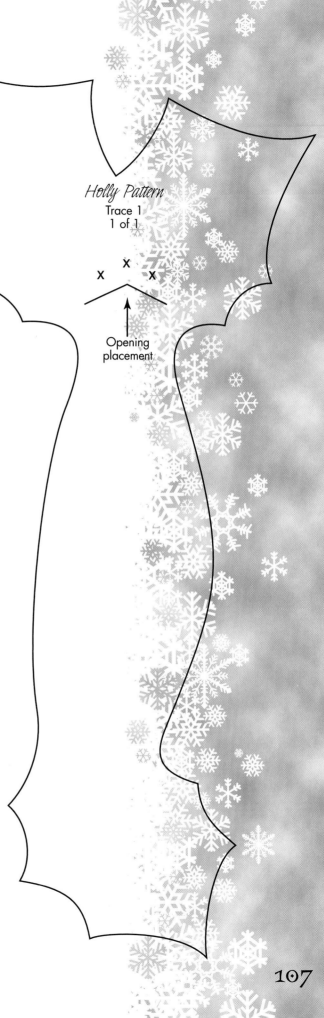

Holly Pattern
Trace 1
1 of 1

x   x   x

↑
Opening
placement

Holly Napkin Ring

1 *Pattern:* Trace the pattern to tracing paper, and cut out. Place pattern on the non-desired side of Ultrasuede, and trace around it onto the fabric with a pen. Mark the opening as indicated on the pattern.

2 *Cutting:* Cut out the holly pattern with scissors. See the Step 2 illustration to make a slit for the opening at the center with the craft knife, cutting from the center outward.

3 *Finishing:* Stitch wooden bead berries with red thread to the right side of the Ultrasuede, following the 3 X's marked on the pattern. Slip the single holly leaf end through the slit to form a ring.

How to Fold Napkin

See the Napkin A illustration to fold the square napkin diagonally to make a triangle with the fold at the lower edge. See the B illustration to fold the lower corners in to the center. Roll the folded edges in to the center, making 2 tubes meeting in the middle.

Napkin

A
Fold

B
Fold   Fold

HOLIDAY Home dec

Materials

FOR BOTH PROJECTS
- All-purpose primer
- Varnish

FOR PICTURE FRAME
- 6½" x 8" (16.3 x 20.5 cm) wood frame with 3½" x 5" (9 x 12.5 cm) opening
- Wooden stars: two 1" (2.5 cm); 1¾" (4.5 cm)
- Acrylic paints: medium blue, white, red, green
- Flat paintbrushes: ¼" (6 mm), ½" (1.3 cm)
- 6" (15 cm) cinnamon stick
- Pattern Page 175

FOR SWITCH PLATE
- Wooden switch plate with beveled edges.
- Wooden shapes: 3" (7.5 cm) heart, ½" (1.3 cm) button
- Acrylic paints: mauve, spruce, white, black, ivory, beige, blush
- Paintbrushes: ¾" (2 cm) flat, No. 10/0 liner, ½" (1.3 cm) rake, texture or scruffy
- 4" (10 cm) jute
- Miscellaneous items: sandpaper, tack cloth, tracing and graphite paper, ruler, pencil, paint palette, utility knife, white craft glue, toothpick, stylus

Make these easy projects for your own home, or for a gift sure to delight. santa smiles on the holiday plaid switch plate, while a photo of your loved ones is the center of attention in a christmas tree picture frame.

1   *Preparation:* Refer to Painting Instructions and Techniques on page 160. Let paint dry between colors and coats. Apply 1 coat of primer to all wood surfaces with a flat brush. Sand lightly to smooth, and remove dust with a tack cloth.

 2   *Pattern:* Trace the picture frame pattern to tracing paper; transfer to the frame with graphite paper and a pencil. Do not do the inner frame edge design lines yet.

 3   *Frame Basecoat:* Use the flat brushes to basecoat the sky with blue, the Christmas tree with green, the stars and inner frame opening edge with red and the snow with white. Extend the paint onto the frame edges. Transfer the inner frame edge lines or use the ¼" (6 mm) brush to paint freehand white stripes on the inner frame edge; see the Step 3 illustration. Dot snowflakes randomly with white.

 4   *Finishing Frame:* Sand the edges of the stars and frame to give them a distressed appearance; remove dust with a tack cloth. Apply a coat of varnish to the entire frame. Use the utility knife to cut the cinnamon stick into graduated lengths to fit the trunk. Refer to the photo and the Step 4 illustration to glue the cinnamon sticks to the painted trunk. Glue the stars to the frame.

5   *Switch Plate Basecoat:* Use the flat brush to basecoat the switch plate with beige and the edges with mauve. Refer to the photo to basecoat the heart Santa's face with blush, the hat with mauve, the hat cuff and beard with ivory and the button with spruce, extending paint on the edges.

 6   *Switch Plate Details:* Use a toothpick to dot the eyes with black. Use the pencil eraser to dot Santa's beard with white. Refer to the photo and Step 6 illustration to use the rake brush to paint mauve vertical lines and spruce horizontal lines about 1" (2.5 cm) apart on the switch plate.

 7   *Finishing Switch Plate:* Tie a small jute bow. Refer to the photo to glue Santa to the switch plate and the button and jute bow to his hat. Use the flat brush to apply varnish to the finished switch plate.

Step 3 – Picture Frame

Step 4 – Picture Frame

Step 6 – Switch Plate

Gardener's wreath

a wreath that proclaims your favorite hobby to all who visit your home for the holidays might also make a great gift for the gardener on your shopping list.

Materials

- 14" (35.5 cm) narrow vine wreath (with vine bows, optional)
- Artificial greenery: 48" (122 cm) mixed pine garland, 6 holly picks, 4 mistletoe picks
- Red velvet craft ribbon: 1/2 yd. (0.5 m), 1" (2.5 cm) wide; 3/4 yd. (0.7 m), 2 1/2" (6.5 cm) wide
- 8 yd. (7.35 m) green jute twine
- Twenty-four 24" (61 cm) lengths natural raffia

- Three 8" (20.5 cm) mini garden tools
- Four 2" (5 cm) terra-cotta pots with drainage holes
- Acrylic paints: red, green
- 1/2" (1.3 cm) sponge brush
- Two 1/2" (1.3 cm) gold jingle bells
- Wires: 16" (40.5 cm) heavy gold, 26-gauge floral paddle
- Miscellaneous items: wire cutters, scissors, ruler, hot glue gun

Step 1

24" pine garland

14"

7"

Step 3

Top bow

Bottom bow

 1   *Preparation:* Determine top of wreath. Make a 26-gauge wire hanging loop on top back. Cut 24" (61 cm) of pine garland and center on top front of wreath; wire and hot-glue in place. Cut two 7" (18 cm) pieces from remaining garland, and wire and glue to bottom front of wreath, as seen in the Step 1 illustration. Use sponge brush to paint terra-cotta pots red on the inside and outside, and handles of mini garden tools green; let dry.

2   *Making Bows:* Wire all bows around the center with 26-gauge craft wire. Tie 1" (2.5 cm) velvet ribbon into a 2-loop bow with 2 1/2" (6.5 cm) loops. Tie 2 1/2" (6.5 cm) velvet ribbon into a 2-loop bow with 4" (10 cm) loops. Cut a V in each streamer end. Use 8 strands of raffia each to make 2 large raffia bows with 4" (10 cm) loops. Use 4 strands of raffia each to make 2 small raffia bows with 3" (7.5 cm) loops. Cut five 1-yd. (0.95 m) lengths of green twine and tie each into a 6-loop bow with 2 1/2" (6.5 cm) loops. Tie remaining twine into a 10-loop bow with 3" (7.5 cm) loops.

3   *Assembling Bows:* See the Step 3 illustration to cut 20" (51 cm) of wire and layer the large red velvet bow, the large green twine bow and a large raffia bow. Wire the 3 together, and then to bottom front of wreath. Repeat to layer the remaining large raffia bow, small red velvet bow and a small green twine bow; wire to top front of wreath. Wire small raffia bows to each side of wreath. Wire green twine bows above and below small raffia bows.

Step 5

4   *Pot Bells:* Cut gold wire in half, and thread each piece through jingle bell, centering the bell on the wire. Knot ends together 1 1/2" (3.8 cm) above the bell, thread ends through hole in pot and knot again on outside of pot. Jingle bell should hang like bell clapper inside pot. Wire pot bells just below bows at top of wreath.

5   *Berry Picks:* Hot-glue 1 cluster of mistletoe and 1 sprig of pine in each remaining pot. See the Step 5 illustration to hot-glue a pot to each side of wreath between green twine bows. Glue remaining mistletoe on either side of bottom bow. Glue a holly cluster above and below top bow. Glue remaining holly clusters on each side of top bow.

 6   *Finishing:* Wire garden tools together at center and fan apart. Cut a small piece of pine, and wrap around center to cover wire. Wire and glue tools to center of bottom bow.

SNOWMAN afGHAN

Materials

- 100% acrylic worsted-weight yarn, 3.5-oz. (100 g) skeins: 8 light blue; 6 white; 1 each: red, green, black
- Size F crochet hook or size needed to obtain gauge
- 1¼" (3.2 cm) black pom-pom
- Miscellaneous items: scissors, ruler, tapestry needle, black sewing thread, steam iron, press cloth

1. *Preparation:* Refer to the Crochet Stitches and Abbreviations on page 162. *Gauge:* Each square = 1⅞" (4.7 cm) *Finished Size:* Approximately 37½" x 48" (95.3 x 122 cm). The afghan requires a total of 500 squares.

2. *Single-Color Squares:* Make 237 blue, 167 white, 16 black, 12 red and 8 green squares. For each square, ch 5, sl st to form a ring. *Rnd 1:* (wrong side) Ch 3 (counts as dc), 2 dc in ring. * Ch 3, 3 dc in ring (corner made). Rep from * twice. Ch 3, sl st into third ch of ch-3, turn. *Rnd 2:* (right side) [Ch 3 (counts as dc), 2 dc, ch 3, 3 dc] in ch-3 sp (corner made). * Ch 1, (3 dc, ch 3, 3 dc) in next corner. Rep from * twice. Ch 1, sl st in 3rd ch of beg ch-3. Fasten off and weave in ends.

this playful snowman will become your little one's favorite cuddle-time buddy. even a beginning crocheter can make this—all from one basic granny square.

3 *Eye Squares:* Make 2. Rep Rnd 1 of Step 2 with white. Fasten off.
Rnd 2: With black, join with a sl st in any ch-3 sp and rep Rnd 2 of Step 2.

 4 *2-Color Squares:* Use 1 color in the square as Color A and the other as Color B. Crochet 19 white/blue, 14 red/green, 10 white/black, 5 blue/green, 4 white/red, 3 blue/red, and 2 black/blue squares. With A, ch 5, sl st to form a ring.
Rnd 1: (wrong side) Ch 3 (counts as dc), 2 dc in ring, ch 3, 3 dc in ring (corner made). Drop A, but do not cut the yarn. Draw B through lp on hook (1 ch made), ch 2, 3 dc in ring, ch 3, 3 dc in ring. Ch 3, join with a sl st in third ch of ch-3 of A, turn.
Rnd 2: (right side) 2 sl st in ch-3 sp, ch 3 (counts as dc), 2 dc in same sp, ch 1 (3 dc, ch 3, 3 dc) in next ch-3 corner. Ch 1, 3 dc, ch 3. Drop B. With A, work 3 dc in next corner. Ch 1, 3 dc, ch 3. Join with a sl st in third ch of ch-3 of B. Fasten off both colors and weave in ends.

5 *3-Color Squares:* Make 1, found at the left shoulder. Ch 5 with blue, sl st to form a ring.
Rnd 1: (wrong side) Ch 3 (counts as dc), 2 dc in ring, ch 3, 3 dc in ring (corner made). Drop blue, but do not cut the yarn. Draw red through lp on hook, ch 2, 3 dc in ring. Drop red, but do not cut the yarn. Draw green through lp on hook, ch 2, 3 dc in ring, ch 3. Join with a sl st in third ch of ch-3 of blue, turn.
Rnd 2: (right side) 2 sl st in ch-3 sp, ch 3 (counts as dc), 2 dc in same sp, ch 1, 3 dc in next ch-3 corner, ch 3, drop green. With red, work 3 dc in same ch-3 corner, ch 1, 3 dc in next corner, ch 3, drop red. With blue, work 3 dc in next ch-3 corner. Ch 1 (3 dc, ch 3, 3 dc) in next ch-3 corner. Ch 1, 3 dc in next corner, ch 3. Join with a sl st in third ch of ch-3 of green. Fasten off all colors.

 6 *Assembly:* Refer to the Assembly Guide. Use the yarn needle and matching yarn to whipstitch the squares right sides together, from corner to corner, stitching in the outer loops only. Stitch the squares together in rows, then stitch the rows together. Cover the afghan with a press cloth and iron with a steam iron.

 7 *Details:* Sew the pom-pom nose to the face with matching thread. Use double strands of black yarn to make a 6¼" (15.7 cm) chain for the pipe stem. Use matching thread to tack in place from the mouth to the pipe bowl. Cut twenty 6" (15 cm) lengths each of red and green yarn for the scarf fringe. Using 2 strands of the same color, fold the yarn in half, and with a crochet hook, loop them through the bottom stitches of the scarf ends, alternating colors. Trim even.

Afghan Assembly Guide

Afghan Color Key

☐	Lt. Blue	■ (gray)	Green
☐	White	■	Black
■	Red		

Pine piLLow

a simpLe triangLe piLLow becomes an eLegant christmas tree, when made of a decorator fabric and embeLLished with goLd braid trim and pearL beads.

Materials

- ½" (1.3 cm) green tone-on-tone decorator fabric, such as velour, velvet, taffeta, etc., 45" (115 cm) wide
- 2 yd. (1.85 m) gold braid trim, ⅜" to ½" (1 to 1.3 cm) wide
- Polyester fiberfill
- 7 pearl beads, ¼" (6 mm) diameter
- ¾" (2 cm) or larger gold star-shaped button
- Miscellaneous items: 18" (46 cm) square tracing or pattern paper, pencil, chalk pencil, yardstick, scissors, rotary cutter and mat (optional), straight pins, sewing machine and matching threads, iron, sewing needle

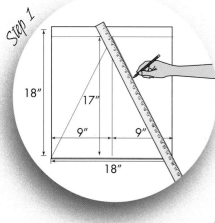

Step 1

1 *Pattern:* See the Step 1 illustration to draw the tree pattern on tracing or pattern paper. Make an 18" (46 cm) line along the top and bottom of the paper. Mark the center points of each line, at 9" (23 cm). Draw a 17" (43 cm) line perpendicular to the 18" (46 cm) lines by drawing through the marked center points. Draw lines from the end points of the bottom 18" (46 cm) line to the top of the 17" (43 cm) line to make a triangle.

 2 *Cutting:* Place the pattern on the decorator fabric, and pin, as seen in the Step 2 illustration. Use the 17" (43 cm) line as a grainline. Cut 2 triangles; this layout will take care of nap in velour and velvet fabrics.

3 *Trim Placement Lines:* Follow the Step 3 illustration to mark trim placement lines in numerical order with a chalk pencil on the right side of one triangle fabric piece. Draw lines 1 and 2, making them 2½" (6.5 cm) in from each edge. Draw lines 3 and 4 as shown, 4" (10 cm) in from the first two lines, and lines 5 and 6 another 4" (10 cm) in.

4 *Stitching Trim:* Place the trim on the marked triangle, beginning with lines 5 and 6. Glue-baste or pin trim in place, cutting the trim only after it is pinned or glued. Set the machine with a medium stitch length and zigzag stitch, down the center of each trim piece. Repeat to pin and stitch, trim lines 4, 3, 2 and 1, in that order.

 5 *Pearl Beads:* Hand-stitch a pearl bead where indicated on the Step 3 illustration by a yellow dot, at each gold braid trim intersection. Stitch through each pearl bead at least 2 times. There will be 1 remaining bead for the star topper.

6 *Pillow Assembly:* Pin the decorated pillow front to the pillow back, right sides together and raw edges matching. Stitch all around with a ½" (1.3 cm) seam allowance, leaving 5" (12.5 cm) open at the bottom for turning and filling. Backstitch at the beginning and end of stitching. Trim seam allowances at points. Press seam allowance open lightly; turn right side out.

 7 *Finishing:* Hand-stitch the remaining pearl bead to the center of the star button; stitch the button to the top of the pillow for the star tree topper. Stuff the pillow with fiberfill, making sure to firmly stuff each corner first. Slipstitch the opening shut.

Step 2

45"

18"

Step 3

1   2

3   4   2½"

5   6

4"

sentimental
Mitten plaque

Crackling and antiquing give this plaque a time-worn look while microwavable plaster gives it a modern twist. the sentiment of a mother's love and care will always be appreciated.

Materials

- 6" x 9" (15 x 23 cm) beveled-edge wooden plaque
- Acrylic paints: French vanilla, blue, red, black
- Paintbrushes: 1" (2.5 cm) sponge, No. 4 shader, No. 10/1 liner
- Crackle medium*
- Plaster products*: 16-oz. (500 mL) bottle microwavable plaster, 1¾" x 3⅛" (4.5 x 7.8 cm) mitten mold and mustard, burgundy, blue plaster paints*: Note: a 2" x 3" (5 x 7.5 cm) wooden mitten could also be purchased and painted instead.
- Waterbase satin varnish*
- Brown antiquing medium*
- 1¾" (4.5 cm) sawtooth hanger with nails
- Assorted trims: 6" (15 cm) natural raffia, ¾" (2 cm) ivory flat button
- Pattern Page 163
- Miscellaneous items: sandpaper, tack cloth, tracing and transfer paper, pencil, paint palette, plastic bowl, measuring spoons, microwave oven, fine-line black permanent-ink marker, natural sponge, soft cloth, white craft glue, hammer

*(See Sources on pg. 176 for purchasing information.)

1 *Basecoating:* Refer to the Painting Instructions and Techniques on page 160. Let paint dry between coats and colors. Sand the wooden plaque smooth; remove dust with the tack cloth. Use the sponge brush to basecoat the plaque front with blue. Paint the beveled edge with red.

2 *Crackling:* Use the sponge brush and follow the manufacturer's instructions to apply 1 coat of crackle medium to the plaque front. Let dry 2 to 4 hours; then paint with 1 coat of French vanilla; see the Step 2 illustration. Do not overlap or restroke the vanilla paint when painting over the crackle medium.

3 *Painting Design:* Trace the pattern to tracing paper, and cut out. Transfer pattern to the plaque front. Use the liner brush to paint the letters and dot the ends with black. Refer to the Step 3 illustration to paint the hearts with blue and the dashed lines with red. Use the sponge brush to varnish the entire plaque.

4 *Mitten:* Follow the manufacturer's instructions to mix 2 tablespoons (25 mL) of plaster with 3 teaspoons (15 mL) of water in a plastic bowl. Pour the plaster into the mold; dry in the microwave oven. Use the shader brush to paint the mitten center with blue, the heart and border with burgundy and the cuff with mustard. Use the black marker to draw in the mitten stitches.

5 *Antiquing:* Use the sponge to apply antiquing medium to the entire plaque and the mitten. Wipe off the excess with a soft cloth.

6 *Finishing:* Nail the hanger to the top back, centered widthwise. Glue the mitten to the center front of the plaque. Tie a 1" (2.5 cm) raffia bow; trim the ends. Refer to the photo and the Step 6 illustration to glue the bow and button to the mitten.

Harvest
waLL hanging

In scandinavian countries, a decorative sheaf of grains is put outside for the birds to enjoy during the holiday season as well as to decorate the house. continue this tradition, inside, with a waLL hanging made of LocaLLy avaiLaBLe grains and a pLaid bow.

Materials

- Dried naturals, available outdoors locally or at floral and craft stores: 1 bunch of 24" to 26" (61 to 66 cm) brizza maxima or other natural-colored grains/plant materials, such as wheat or oats;1 bunch of 20" (51 cm) black beard wheat or other natural-colored grains/plant materials; 10 pieces each cranberry wild oats and dried green plant; dyed Princess pine or preserved cedar

- 24-gauge floral wire

- 1½ yd. (1.4 m) red/green plaid with gold wire-edged ribbon, 2½" (6.5 cm) wide

- 1 yd. (0.95 m) gold cord

- Miscellaneous items: ruler, scissors, hot glue gun

1 *Base:* Place the longest plant material, the brizza maxima, on a flat work surface. Grasp the bunch near the center, and use both hands to fan it out; see the Step 1 illustration. Cut 12" (30.5 cm) of wire, twist tightly around the center to hold the fan shape, and trim the wire ends.

Step 1

2 *Wheat:* Repeat Step 1 for the shorter black beard wheat, but cut 18" (46 cm) of wire. Place the wheat on the brizza maxima base, and twist the wire around both bundles to secure them together. Do not cut the excess wire yet, but use it to form a 1" (2.5 cm) hanging loop in the back.

3 *Bow:* Make a bow by following the Step 3 illustration. Begin with a 13" (33 cm) streamer, then form two 6" (15 cm) loops, a 2" (5 cm) center loop and another 13" (33 cm) streamer. Each time the ribbon passes through the center, pinch and twist it tightly to narrow the center down. Cut 12" (30.5 cm) of wire, and twist it around the bow where you have pinched it.

Step 3

2"
6"

Bow side view

13"

Start   Finish

4 *Attaching Bow:* Place the bow on the plant material, and bring the wire around to the back, twist tightly, and tuck the ends in to secure. Shape the center loop to hide the wire. Shape the other loops and the streamers to look as shown in the photo, or as desired. The wire-edged ribbon is very easy to form into beautiful shapes. Cut V's in the streamer ends.

5 *Red and Green Naturals:* Break or cut the stems of cranberry-colored oats and green naturals into 4" to 6" (10 to 15 cm) pieces. Place them on either side of the bow, with the stem ends tucked into the bow or other naturals to hide; hot-glue the pieces into place. Hot-glue shorter sprigs of Princess pine or preserved cedar on top of the red and green naturals.

Step 6

6 *Gold Cord:* Cut the gold cord in half. Run the cord through the center loop, and arrange on top of the streamer below the loop and onto the naturals above the loop; refer to the photo and the Step 6 illustration. Hot-glue as needed to keep the cord shaped and hold in place.

Countdown calendar

An easy-to-make countdown calendar gets everyone in the holiday spirit during the month of December. Spot will love getting a tasty biscuit each day from his puppy treat tree. A cat or a child would be equally thrilled with his or her favorite treat.

Materials

- Felt: 2/3 yd. (0.63 m) 36" (91.5 cm) green, 9" x 12" (23 x 30.5 cm) square gold
- Assorted trims: 9" (23 cm) red picot satin ribbon, 1/4" (6 mm) wide; two each 1/2" (1.3 cm) brass jingle bells and mini pinecones; 7 silk holly leaves
- Natural raffia and 1 wood craft stick

- 7" (18 cm) jute twine
- 24 small- to medium-size dog biscuits or treats
- Glues: hot glue gun, white craft glue
- Pattern Sheet
- Miscellaneous items: tracing paper, pencil, scissors, straight pins, sewing machine and matching threads, ruler

Step 2

1 *Patterns:* Trace the 7 patterns, and cut out as indicated from felt. Use craft glue to glue 2 gold stars together.

2 *Assembly:* Place tree pieces together, and pin. Refer to the photo and the Step 2 illustration to pin 5 pocket strips in place. Stitch a 1/4" (6 mm) seam around the outer edge of tree; see red stitches in the Step 3 illustration.

Step 3

Contrasting thread used to show stitches

1/4" seam =
1/8" seam =
pockets =

3 *Pocket Strips:* Sew a 1/8" (3 mm) seam across the bottom of each pocket strip except for the bottom one; see the blue stitches in the Step 3 illustration. Topstitch the yellow lines as indicated, creating 24 pockets, each approximately 1 3/4" (4.5 cm) wide.

4 *Decorating:* Hot-glue star to top of tree. Fill each pocket with a biscuit or treat. Refer to the photo to hot-glue 3 holly leaf clusters to tree. Cut red ribbon into three 3" (7.5 cm) pieces. Tie 3 small red bows; glue bow to each leaf cluster. Glue a bell or pinecones to each cluster.

Step 5

5 *Trunk & Hanging Loop:* Glue craft stick to tree back with 1" (2.5 cm) of stick extending at center bottom edge; see the Step 5 illustration. Tie a 7" (18 cm) raffia bow, and glue to stick. Tie jute twine hanging loop, and glue to top back of tree.

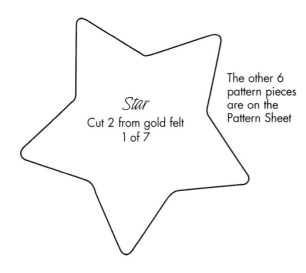

Star
Cut 2 from gold felt
1 of 7

The other 6 pattern pieces are on the Pattern Sheet

wear a
Poinsettia

Clustered around the holiday's perennial favorite flower—the poinsettia, are branches of pine, sprigs of mistletoe and holly leaves accented with bead berries. tie the nosegay together with a bow and in just a stitch of time, you've created a wardrobe essential for the holidays!

Materials

- White cotton blouse
- Embroidery ribbon:
  7 mm: 3 yd. (2.75 m) each fern green (020) and red (539);
  4 mm: 3 yd. (2.75 m) each forest green (628), sunflower (666), brown (671)
- 1 skein each 6-strand embroidery floss: Vy. Dk. Pistachio Green No. 319, Vy. Dk. Olive Green No. 730
- Needles: No. 18 chenille, sewing
- 1/3 yd. (0.32 m) red/green/gold Christmas ribbon, 1/4" (6 mm) wide
- Beads: fifteen 2 mm pearls; three 4 mm red
- Miscellaneous items: tracing paper, fine-line black marker, water-soluble transfer pen, scissors, ruler, white sewing thread, iron

*Wear a Poinsettia
Embroidery Guide*

Bow Placement

1 *Pattern:* Trace the Embroidery Guide to tracing paper with the black marker. Refer to the photo to position tracing inside the shirt below the left shoulder. Use the transfer pen to trace over the lines onto the shirt front.

2 *Stitching:* Refer to the Ribbon Embroidery Instructions and Stitches on page 158 and the Embroidery Guide to work the stitches using 12" (30.5 cm) lengths of ribbon or 3 strands of floss. Work the stems of the mistletoe and pine, then the leaves and needles.

3 *Holly:* Use 4 mm Forest Green Ribbon No. 628 to work slightly slanted satin stitches from the center outward to fill in the leaves. Work Vy. Dk. Pistachio Green No. 319 floss stem stitches for the center veins and stems.

4 *Poinsettia:* Work Japanese ribbon stitches and straight stitches for petals, being careful not to pull the ribbon too tight and letting it twist slightly on some straight stitches. Work the longer petals first, then fill in with shorter petals to give the flower dimension. Make the sunflower French knots at the center.

5 *Finishing:* Tie the Christmas ribbon in a small bow. Use white sewing thread to tack the bow to the bouquet stems and sew the beads where indicated.

*Wear a Poinsettia
Color/Stitch Key*

MISTLETOE		
⌒	730	Vy. Dk. Olive Green Floss Stem Stitch (stems)
⬭	020	7 mm Fern Green Ribbon Straight Stitch (leaves)
⊕		2 mm Pearl Bead
PINE		
⁓	671	4 mm Brown Ribbon Stem Stitch (stems)
╱	628	4 mm Forest Green Ribbon Straight Stitch (needles)
HOLLY		
╱	319	Vy. Dk. Pistachio Green Floss Stem Stitch (veins and stems)
●		4 mm Red Bead
POINSETTIA		
╱	539	7 mm Red Ribbon Japanese Ribbon and Straight Stitches (petals)
O	666	4 mm Sunflower Ribbon French Knot (flower center)

female frosty

PAINTED ON EVER-VERSATILE CLAY POTS, this rosy-cheeked snow figure has an old-fashioned, friendly charm that will appeal to everyone.

Materials

- Terra-cotta pots: 4" (10 cm), 5½" (14 cm)
- Brush-on acrylic primer
- Acrylic paints: mauve, green, white, black, ivory, yellow ochre
- Textured snow paint
- Satin varnish
- Paintbrushes: old scruffy, ¾" (2 cm) flat, No. 10/0 liner, spatter, small stencil, 1" (2.5 cm) sponge, sea sponge
- ½" (1.3 cm) checkerboard stencil
- Wooden cutouts: 2½" (6.5 cm) bird, 1½" (3.8 cm) heart
- Small tree twigs for arms
- 6" (15 cm) black felt hat
- Spanish moss
- ⅔ yd. (0.63 m) green satin sheen paper ribbon
- Glues: thick white craft, hot glue gun
- Miscellaneous items: sandpaper, tack cloth, paint palette, paper towels, drill with ¼" bit

1 *Preparation:* Wash the pots to remove dust. Let them dry thoroughly. Apply primer to the pots using a sponge brush. Let dry between paint coats and colors. Refer to the Painting Instructions and Techniques on page 160.

 2 *Basecoating:* Sand the pots to rough them up to allow the paint to adhere. Remove dust with a tack cloth. Using the sponge brush, basecoat the pots with 2 or 3 coats of ivory. Paint the bird and heart with mauve. Paint the beak with yellow ochre. Sand the paint off of the edges of the wooden shapes for a weathered look.

 3 *Eyes & Mouth:* Refer to the photo. Dot 3 buttons with black paint down the center front of the body pot and 2 small dots for eyes on the head pot. Dot the mouth center; then continue the dots toward 1 side of the face without re-dipping to create dots of diminishing size. Re-dip the handle into black, dot once on the palette, then repeat to dot the other side of the mouth. Dot an eye on the bird.

4 *Nose & Cheeks:* Load the liner brush with mauve; see the Step 4 illustration. Working from the center of the face, stroke the brush back and forth to form a carrot-shaped nose. Load the stencil brush with mauve and dry-brush the cheeks.

5 *Border & Arms:* Load the stencil brush with green. Using the checkerboard stencil, stencil checks on the rim of the large pot. Drill a hole on opposite sides 2" (5 cm) from the flat bottom for the arms, as shown in the Step 5 illustration. Hot-glue the branches into the holes, holding in place until secure. Hot-glue the small pot on top of the large pot.

 6 *Decorations:* Glue the heart to the pot. Use thinned black paint and the liner brush to paint stitch lines on the pot near the heart. Use the sea sponge to sponge white highlights onto the pots. Thin white paint with water to an ink-like consistency. Then spatter the snow woman with the thinned paint.

 7 *Scarf:* Untwist the ribbon and paint 1" (2.5 cm) mauve stripes, 2" (5 cm) apart. Load the liner brush with white and paint "stitch" lines on either side of the mauve stripes. Using the flat brush, apply 1 to 2 coats of varnish to the pots and the scarf. Place and glue the paper ribbon scarf around the neck.

8 *Finishing:* Hot-glue Spanish moss to the top of the head for the hair, as shown in the Step 8 illustration. Glue the hat on the head. Hot-glue a moss "nest" to the top of the hat and the bird in the nest. Use an old scruffy brush to apply the textured snow paint as desired to the hat, arms, scarf and pots.

winter's fragrances

these easy-to-make formulas are wonderful ways to pamper yourself and those you care about.

Materials

FOR PEPPERMINT MILK BATH

- 1 tablespoon (15 mL) dried peppermint leaves
- ½ cup (125 mL) powdered milk
- Small glass jar with cork or lid

FOR BAYBERRY SOAP SPONGE

- 4-oz. (125 g) bar unscented white soap*
- 15 drops bayberry fragrance oil*
- 1 yd. (0.95 m) burgundy bridal tulle
- 1 yd. (0.95 m) burgundy satin ribbon, ¼" (6 mm) wide

FOR WINTER ROMANCE PERFUME

- 1 tablespoon (15 mL) grated beeswax*
- 4 teaspoons (20 mL) mineral oil
- Fragrance oils*: 10 drops each lavender, lemon, rose
- Small metal tin or plastic container with tight-fitting lid or cap

FOR FRANKINCENSE & MYRRH SOAP

- 4-oz. (125 g) bar unscented glycerin soap*
- Fragrance oils*: 10 drops each frankincense and myrrh
- ⅛ teaspoon (0.5 mL) gold mica dust*
- Soap mold*

FOR CHAMPAGNE BUBBLE BATH

- ¼ cup (50 mL) foaming concentrate*
- ½ teaspoon (2 mL) table salt
- 1 tablespoon (15 mL) glycerin*
- Fragrance oils*: 15 drops each sage, chamomile, pink grapefruit
- Clean empty champagne split bottle with cap or cork
- Fine-point pink paint pen, gold seal stickers
- Miscellaneous items: measuring spoons and cups, mortar and pestle or coffee grinder, mixing spoons and bowls, food processor or cheese grater, small saucepan, stove, small oven-safe bowl, clear cellophane, scissors

*(See Sources on pg. 176 for purchasing information.)

Peppermint Milk Bath

A CREAMY PEPPERMINT MILK BATH COMBINES THE
SKIN-NOURISHING EFFECTS OF MILK WITH AROMATHERAPEUTIC PEPPERMINT.

Crush the peppermint leaves into a fine powder using the mortar and pestle. Mix with powdered milk together in a bowl until well blended. Store the milk bath in a glass jar or other closed container in a cool, dry place.

Bayberry Soap Sponge

BRIDAL TULLE WRAPS UP BAYBERRY-SCENTED SOAP
FOR A GREAT EXFOLIATING BATH SPONGE.

Use a food processor to shred the soap into slivers. Place the shredded soap into a bowl and add the bayberry oil; stir until well blended. Let the scented soap air dry for 3 hours, then restir. Fold the tulle again and again into an 8" or 9" (20.5 or 23 cm) square. Place the scented soap slivers into the center of the square, then bring the corners of the tulle up around the soap to form a bag, as shown in the illustration. Knot the ribbon tightly around the tulle to secure the soap inside, then tie the ribbon ends together 1" (2.5 cm) from the end to form a hanging loop.

Winter Romance Perfume

THE WINTER ROMANCE PERFUME IS IN A SOLID BASE,
MAKING IT PERFECT TO TUCK IN YOUR PURSE.

Boil 1" (2.5 cm) of water in a saucepan. Place the beeswax and mineral oil into an oven-safe bowl; place the bowl in saucepan. Stir until wax dissolves, then remove from the heat. See the illustration to stir in the fragrance oils and pour into a small container. Let set for 2 hours to solidify.

Frankincense & Myrrh Soap

GOLD MICA DUST MAKES THE
FRANKINCENSE AND MYRRH SOAP GLISTEN AND GLEAM.

Melt the glycerin soap in a saucepan over low heat, stirring constantly until liquefied. Remove from the heat and add the fragrance oils and mica dust; stir until evenly colored. See the illustration to pour the mixture into a mold; let set until hard. Wrap the soap in clear cellophane.

Champagne Bubble Bath

NEW YEAR'S WOULDN'T BE COMPLETE
WITHOUT THE WHIMSICAL DELIGHT OF A CHAMPAGNE BUBBLE BATH.

Mix the foaming concentrate and 3/4 cup (175 mL) water in a bowl, stirring gently until well blended. Add the salt and stir; the mixture will thicken immediately. Stir in the glycerin and fragrance oils until well blended. Pour the bubble bath into the champagne bottle and seal with a cap or cork. Use the pink paint pen and the gold stickers to label the front and back of the bottle.

Bayberry Soap Sponge

Winter Romance Perfume

Frankincense & Myrrh Soap

127

Christmas tree
cuties

Materials

- 6" x 12" (15 x 30.5 cm) ½" (1.3 cm) pine wood
- Acrylic satin varnish or finish
- Acrylic paints: green sea, hunter green, river green, white, silver pine, black, burnt sienna, red, lt. blue, yellow, 14K gold
- Sparkling gold fabric paint
- Acrylic blending medium
- Paintbrushes: Nos. 2, 6, 8 and 12 flat; Nos. 0 and 1 liner; old scruffy
- 10" (25.5 cm) metallic gold cord
- Tools: scroll saw, drill with ¹⁄₁₆" drill bit
- Miscellaneous items: tracing and white graphite paper, pencil, stylus, fine sandpaper, tack cloth, paint palette, paper towels, scissors, white craft glue

a couple of basic brush strokes is all it takes to paint this darling duo quick as a wink. their smiling faces and quirky shape will brighten any tree.

128

1 *Preparation:* Trace the pattern to tracing paper, and cut out. Place the pattern on the wood, and trace around twice to make 2 trees, reversing the pattern on the second. Cut out each wood piece. Drill a hole for the hanging loop in the top edge of the tree near the star; refer to the photo.

2 *Basecoating:* Refer to Painting Instructions and Techniques on page 160. Sand the wood smooth and remove dust with a tack cloth. Seal the wood with varnish. Let varnish and paints dry between coats and colors. Use the No. 12 flat brush to basecoat the tree with green sea and the star with 14K gold. Paint the star with sparkling gold fabric paint.

3 *Shading:* Use the graphite paper and stylus to transfer the pattern scallop lines only to the trees. Follow the blending medium manufacturer's instructions to use with paints for all shading and highlighting. Use the appropriate brush size for the area being painted. Shade along the outside edges and under the star and scallops with hunter green. Deepen the shading with river green.

4 *Highlighting:* Mix together 1 part white with 2 parts silver pine and highlight above the scallops, as seen in the Step 4 illustration. Dry-brush hunter green on top of the highlighted scallops. Dry-brush over the hunter green dry-brushing with the white/silver pine mixture; then dry-brush random areas above the scallops with white.

5 *Face:* Use the graphite paper and stylus to transfer the detail lines, omitting dots and circles. Transfer an open and a closed eye to 1 tree, but 2 closed eyes to the other tree. Use the liner brushes for all details, and basecoat the nose with 14K gold, then with sparkling gold. Shade above the nose with hunter green. Paint the mouth, eyebrows, closed eyes and a fine line around the top half of the nose with black. Highlight under each closed eye with white. Paint the open eye white; then paint the iris and outline the eye with black. Highlight the iris with a white comma stroke. Use the scruffy brush to dry-brush cheeks with burnt sienna, and then red.

6 *Ornaments:* Transfer the circles to the front of each tree, or paint them freehand. Use the handle end of the No. 1 liner to dot red, lt. blue and yellow randomly; see the Step 6 illustration. Refer to the photo to paint random groups of 3 white dots.

7 *Finishing:* Protect each ornament with satin varnish. Cut gold cord in half. Fold each piece in half, knot the ends in an overhand knot and trim. Apply glue into the drill hole and use the tip of the stylus to push the knot into the hole.

Step 4

Step 6

Drill hole

Tree
Cut 2, reversing 1, from pine wood
1 of 1

Lighted Sphere

Accent your front door, or fill a tree outdoors, with colorful lighted spheres. for a more understated look, use all one color lights, such as clear or red.

Materials

- 12" (30.5 cm) twig or vine ball
- 200 multicolored miniature outdoor lights, two 50-ft. (15 m) strands, with green cords and sockets
- 22-gauge green floral wire
- 18" (46 cm) wire or monofilament fishing line for hanging cord
- Miscellaneous items: small needlenose pliers, pruning shears

1 *Hole:* Look over the twig ball, and select an area that is loosely woven. Use the pruning shears to cut out the twigs, as seen in the Step 1 illustration. Make a hole large enough so you can get your hand in and work inside the ball. Save the twigs or vines that you cut out, to cover up the hole after completing the project.

2 *Arranging:* Plug in 1 light strand. Bring the socket end of 1 of the light strings inside the twig ball. Pull in the rest of the light strand a bit at a time, and push the lights through to the outside of the twig ball, from the inside. Attach the second strand to the first, and continue.

3 *Wiring:* You will need to wire several of the light bulbs to keep them in place, from falling back into the twig ball, or from poking out too far. Do this as you work, rather than waiting until the end. Cut the 22-gauge green wire into several 12" (30.5 cm) lengths. Twist a wire around a light socket, not just the bulb. Twist the socket and wire onto the closest twig that will hold the light in place; a wire may be used for several lights. The needlenose pliers can help to reach and twist the wire more easily; see the Step 3 illustration.

4 *Spacing:* It is best to push the lights through following their natural spacing on the strands. That may mean that you work around and around the sphere, before the lights are all evenly yet randomly spaced throughout, rather than completely finishing a section of the sphere at a time.

5 *Plug:* Allow the plug to hang outside the ball. After you have hung the ball and determined how you will provide electricity, wire the plug in place. See the Step 5 illustration.

6 *Finishing:* When all the lights are wired and inside the ball, wire the twigs that were cut out in Step 1 back in place to cover the hole. Attach wire or monofilament to 2 strong, closely spaced twigs for a hanging loop. Knot the cord and trim the ends. If your strand of lights has all green wire and sockets, except for 1 or 2 end bulbs, such a strand may still be used. Simply take some green sticky floral tape, and cover the white sockets with it. Those tape-covered bulbs will blend right in with the rest.

felt & ribbon ornaments

felt christmas ornaments are simple to stitch and stuff, because the edges need no finishing. embellished with lace, buttons, embroidery and ribbons, they look great!

Materials

FOR 5 FELT ORNAMENTS

- 5" x 8" (12.5 x 20.5 cm) felt each: off-white, tan, medium green, dark green, burgundy, small amount of pink for stocking patches
- Polyester fiberfill
- Embroidery floss: black, lime green, gold, and colors to match each felt
- Embroidery needle
- 4 mm silk ribbon: purple, magenta, ivory, turquoise, pink

- 1¼ yd. (1.15 m) gold braid, ⅛" (3 mm) wide
- Off-white flat lace: 3½" (9 cm) of 1" (2.5 cm) wide for stocking; 4" (10 cm) of ⅝" (1.5 cm) wide for bear
- ½" (1.3 cm) off-white flat two-hole button
- Pattern Page 173
- Miscellaneous items: tracing paper, pencil, chalk pencil, scissors, powdered blush, cotton swab, straight pins

1. *Preparation:* Trace the patterns to tracing paper, and cut out. Cut patterns from felt as indicated; mark dots on 1 felt piece with chalk pencil.

 2. *Embroidery:* Refer to the Embroidery Stitches on page 158 for how to do stitches. Use 3 strands of embroidery floss for all embroidery and work single-wrap French knots. Embroider each ornament on the single marked layer for the ornament front as follows:

Bear: Embroider a black French knot for each eye. Sew off-white button for nose with stitches running vertically. Blush cheeks using cotton swab.

Tree & Wreath: Embroider a French knot with gold floss at each dot on the tree and with lime green floss at each dot on the wreath.

Stocking: Pin the pink toe and heel patches to the stocking front. Use tiny blanket stitches and burgundy floss to embroider the inside edge of each patch to stocking.

Gingerbread: Embroider a black French knot for each eye; blush cheeks using cotton swab. Tie a small turquoise ribbon bow and sew to center front of neck.

3. *Ornament Assembly:* Cut 9" (23 cm) of gold cord. Fold cord in half and pin raw edges between felt layers at top of ornament. Use matching floss and tiny blanket stitches to embroider around entire ornament, catching the cord in the seam, as shown in the Step 3 illustration. Make sure to leave 1/2" (1.3 cm) opening for stuffing; do not cut thread. Stuff firmly with fiberfill. Continue working blanket stitches around opening to meet first stitch. Knot thread and run needle through ornament to hide thread end; cut thread.

 4. *Finishing Bear:* Use off-white floss to run a basting stitch along straight edge of 5/8" (1.5 cm) lace. Pull thread ends to gather. Wrap lace around bear's neck with raw edges at center back. Knot thread and trim ends. Tie a tiny ivory ribbon bow and tack to neck just below nose.

 5. *Finishing Tree:* See the Step 5 illustration to begin at top of trunk and, following the dashed lines on the pattern, wrap purple ribbon around tree up to top, then crisscross back to bottom. Tie ends in a small bow at the top of the trunk.

 6. *Finishing Stocking:* With straight edge of 1" (2.5 cm) lace even with top of stocking, wrap lace around stocking overlapping ends at center back. With off-white floss, sew top edge of lace to top of stocking and raw edges together in back; see the Step 6 illustration. Tie a small pink ribbon bow and tack to center front of lace.

 7. *Finishing Wreath:* Wrap magenta ribbon around wreath at indentations, following the dashed lines on the pattern, beginning and ending at the lower right. Tie ends in a small bow.

Step 3

Step 5

Step 6

Stocking back side

133

snowtime
Wind chime

Purchased wood shapes
make it a breeze to paint and assemble a cute frosty fellow. protected with gloss varnish, the wind chime is durable enough to weather the elements under the eaves of a front porch.

Materials

- 33" (84 cm) metal electrical conduit pipe, 5/8" (1.5 cm) thick
- Tools: hacksaw or tube cutter, drill with 1/8" bit
- Wood shapes: 4" (10 cm) star, 3 1/2" (9 cm) heart, 1 3/4" (4.5 cm) ball knob, 2 1/2" (6.5 cm) ball, 16 mm round bead
- Spray metal primer
- Acrylic craft paints: white, black, orange, green, blue, red, gold
- Paintbrushes: small and medium flat, fine liner
- Clear acrylic spray sealer
- Antique oak wood stain
- Exterior waterbase gloss varnish
- 2 1/2 yd. (2.3 m) black nylon cord
- Red craft foam for scarf, 1/2" x 8 1/2" (1.3 x 21.8 cm)
- Pattern Sheet
- Miscellaneous items: coarse sandpaper, tracing and graphite paper, pencil, paint palette, ruler, scissors, toothpick, black fine-line permanent-ink marker, soft cloth

1 *Cutting & Drilling:* Use the hacksaw to cut one 5" (12.5 cm) chime and four 7" (18 cm) chimes from the pipe. Drill holes from side to side through 1 end of each pipe ½" (1.3 cm) from the end. Sand the drill holes and pipe ends smooth. Drill a hole through the center of the wood ball, star and knob, and through the heart as shown in the Step 1 illustration. Drill a hole in each star point, ½" (1.3 cm) from tips.

2 *Basecoating:* Refer to the Painting Instructions and Techniques on page 160. Let paints and finishes dry between colors and coats. Refer to manufacturer's instructions to use the various finishes and sealers. Spray the pipe chimes with metal primer. Use the medium flat brush to basecoat all sides of the star with gold, the heart and bead with red, the pipes with blue, and the wood ball and knob white.

3 *Snowman:* Trace the patterns to tracing paper. Use graphite paper and a pencil to transfer the face pattern to the wood knob, and the body pattern to the ball. The flat side of the knob will be the bottom of the head. Use the small flat brush to paint the mittens red and the cuffs green. Use the liner brush to paint the nose orange. Dot the eyes, mouth and buttons black; dot white highlights in eyes with a toothpick. Mix a drop of white with red to make pink. Dip your finger in pink, and lightly swirl to blush cheeks.

4 *Details:* Refer to the photo to use liner brush to paint white snowflakes on the chimes. Use the black marker to make stitching lines on the cheeks, and outline and draw details on the mittens and arms. Refer to the photo to draw a dot-and-dash border around the heart and stars, on both sides. On 1 side of the heart write "I Love Winter," and on the other side, refer to the Step 4 illustration to write "Let It Snow."

5 *Finishes:* Lightly spray the head, body, star and heart with acrylic sealer, to prevent the marker from running. Use the medium flat brush to apply wood stain to the same; wipe excess off with a soft cloth. Apply gloss varnish to all the wood pieces and the chimes.

6 *Snowman Assembly:* Cut 40" (102 cm) of nylon cord. Fold the cord in half, and tie a knot 6" (15 cm) from the fold. Thread the cord ends through the head, coming out at the neck; make sure the knot won't go through the head hole. String the body, star center, and bead tightly onto the cord, and tie several knots below the bead. Tie the heart onto the cord 4" (10 cm) below the bead; tie the cord ends into a bow.

7 *Chime Assembly:* Cut five 6" (15 cm) pieces of nylon cord; thread each through chime holes. Match cord ends, and tie a knot ½" (1.3 cm) above the chime; see the Step 7 illustration. Thread the cord ends through the star tip holes, and knot several times; trim the cord ends. Make sure to place the 5" (12.5 cm) chime on the star point directly in front of the snowman.

8 *Scarf:* Cut the ends of the foam strip to fringe. Cut a ½" (1.3 cm) slit in the center of the strip 1½" (3.8 cm) from 1 end. Wrap the scarf around the snowman's neck, and insert the unslit end through the slit to secure.

tannenbaum togs

Materials

FOR GLITTERING TREES SWEATSHIRT
- White sweatshirt
- Glitter fabric paint: jade, sapphire, teal, bright gold
- Dimensional fabric paint: red
- No. 3 fabric paintbrush
- Pointed detail tool or small knife
- 1¼ yd. (1.15 m) red rickrack
- Pattern Page 172

FOR BEADED TREE SWEATSHIRT
- Red sweatshirt
- 9" x 12" (23 x 30.5 cm) green mini print cotton fabric and fusible web
- Fabric paints: green dimensional, clear crystal glitter
- ½" (1.3 cm) flat paintbrush
- Beads: 4 mm faceted crystal, 29; 4 mm faceted red, 20; 6 mm metallic gold, 37; 13 x 6 mm red faceted elongated bicone, 19; 21 x 7 mm red faceted pendant, 5; 14 x 7.5 mm emerald holly leaves, 11
- Miscellaneous items: T-shirt board, tracing paper, iron-on transfer pencil, iron, aluminum foil, straight pins, sewing needle, sewing machine with matching threads (optional), yardstick, pencil, scissors, white craft glue

With the most basic of painting and sewing skills, you can create either of these two sweatshirts featuring a painted or fabric christmas tree.

Glittering Trees Sweatshirt

1 *Preparation:* Wash and dry sweatshirt; do not use fabric softener. Insert T-shirt board in shirt. Trace the pattern onto tracing paper with iron-on transfer pencil, and transfer to sweatshirt. Refer to the photo to randomly transfer several stars to front and sleeve.

2 *Painting:* Let paint dry between colors and coats. Squeeze a 1" (2.5 cm) puddle of glitter paint onto foil. Scoop up paint with brush and refer to the pattern and the Step 2 illustration to gently pat into place for a single thick coat. For clean, sharp edges, use detail tool to push wet paint back inside lines. After completing the trees, do the stars on the front and sleeves. If necessary, a second coat can be applied for more even coverage. Rinse brush in water between colors.

3 *Finishing:* With shirt lying flat, squeeze dimensional fabric paint beads directly onto fabric. Follow manufacturer's suggestions for dot technique and drying times. Place rickrack around design, and pin. Hand-sew in place with a small stitch at every point, or machine-stitch a row down the middle of rickrack.

Beaded Tree Sweatshirt

1 *Preparation:* Wash and dry sweatshirt and fabric. Do not use fabric softener. Follow the manufacturer's instructions to fuse web to wrong side of green fabric. Draw a triangle tree on the paper backing by marking center point on 1 short side. Follow the Step 1 illustration to draw lines from the center point to corners on opposite end.

2 *Painting:* Cut out triangle tree and peel paper backing. Position on shirt front; fuse. Outline tree with green dimensional paint; let dry. Lightly brush tree with clear crystal glitter paint.

3 *1st Garland:* Follow the Beading Guide for Steps 3-5. Thread needle with a 16" (40.5 cm) length of green thread; double the thread and knot ends. Insert needle from wrong side 1" (2.5 cm) from top at left edge of tree. Sew on a holly leaf with a stitch on either side of tip and end with needle on wrong side. Bring needle through and bead the following pattern: 4 mm red, gold, crystal, red bicone, crystal, and gold. Add a 4 mm red and insert needle at right side of tree 2" (5 cm) from top. Slide beads to first knot, letting drape slightly. Sew on holly leaf. Knot on wrong side; trim.

4 *Remaining Garlands:* Repeat Step 3 for the remaining garlands using the following information. See the Beading Guide for where to begin and end garlands.

GARLAND	THREAD LENGTH	# OF BEADING PATTERNS
2nd	20" (51 cm)	2 + 4 mm red
3rd	24" (61 cm)	3 + 4 mm red
4th	28" (71 cm)	4 + 4 mm red
5th	32" (81.5 cm)	5 + 4 mm red

5 *Finishing:* Sew a gold bead at tip of tree. Sew and glue 4 bicone beads in a cross around gold bead. Sew a gold bead and dangling red pendant for 5 ornaments; knot threads on wrong side along the edge of tree between garlands. Sew or glue 5 holly leaves on tree between strings of garland. Tack-stitch or glue garland if desired. On wrong side, dab glue on each thread knot; let dry.

origami
Snowflakes

Materials

FOR 3 ORNAMENTS

- Lightweight or origami paper squares: 4" (10 cm) gold, 5" (12.5 cm) white, 6" (15 cm) white
- 24" (61 cm) thread for hanging loop
- Miscellaneous items: tracing paper, pencil, sharp scissors, iron, sewing needle

Bring back memories from christmas past, and make beautiful paper snowflakes to hang on your tree, use as gift tags or tape on your windows.

1 *Folding into Squares:* Fold paper squares in half, making rectangles. When folding the gold paper, fold the gold color to the inside. Fold the paper in half again to make small squares, each half the size of the original.

2 *Marking:* Refer to the Step 2 illustration and the following table to mark the paper squares into thirds for folding. Place the folded squares with the folds and open edges as shown. Use a pencil and ruler to mark the appropriate distance for the appropriate square from the 4-open-edges corner on each side. Lightly draw the folding lines from the marked points to the opposite corner.

ORIGINAL SQUARE SIZE	FOLDED SQUARE SIZE	DISTANCE TO MARK FROM CORNER
4″ (10 cm)	2″ (5 cm)	7/8″ (2.2 cm)
5″ (12.5 cm)	2½″ (6.5 cm)	1⅛″ (2.8 cm)
6″ (15 cm)	3″ (7.5 cm)	1⅜″ (3.5 cm)

3 *Folding into Thirds:* Refer to the Step 3 illustration to fold the square along the marked lines into thirds. Fold the third along the single fold under; see 3B. Fold the third along the 2 folds up or forward; see 3C. Try to make these folds as accurate as possible.

4 *Trimming:* See the Step 4 illustration to cut off the end to make a triangle or pie shape. Hold the piece as shown, with the double folds away from you. Place the paper well within the scissor blades, aligning along the shortest point on the bottom side and the shortest point on the top side. Cut across; trim to even up, if necessary.

5 *Pattern:* Trace the patterns to tracing paper, and cut out. Trace the pattern lightly with pencil to the top section of the appropriate triangle piece. Use sharp scissors to cut into the folded edges where marked. You may need to use the innermost part of the scissor blades to get enough strength to cut through all the layers.

6 *Finishing:* Carefully open up the cut snowflake, making sure not to tear it. Erase any remaining pencil marks. Press with a warm iron or place in a thick book to flatten. Cut hanging loop thread into three 8″ (20.5 cm) pieces. Thread through a needle, and insert through the end of 1 snowflake point, about ¼″ (6 mm) in. Remove the needle, tie a knot, and trim the ends.

Step 2

4 open edges

6″ square folded to a 3″ square

1⅜″

1⅜″

Folding lines

1 fold

2 double folds

Step 3

Fold under

A

Fold up

B

C

Step 4

6″ Square
Trace 1
1 of 3

5″ Square
Trace 1
2 of 3

4″ Gold Square
Trace 1
3 of 3

Button
boxes

You can bedeck boxes with buttons and pretty trims to make keepsake storage for precious gifts and collectibles.

Materials

- Purchased fabric-covered boxes, your choice, 2" or 4" (5 or 10 cm) square
- 3/8" wide (1 cm) coordinating ribbon and cord: 1/3 yd. (0.32 m) each for small box, 1/2 yd. each (0.5 m) for large box
- Tassels: 1 each small and large
- 1/4" to 3/4" (6 mm to 2 cm) assorted round or oval white buttons: 33 for small box, 150 for large box
- Miscellaneous items: thick white craft glue, sewing needle and thread

1 *Box Trims:* Begin gluing cord to box lid in back, gently rounding corners. It may help to hold cord in place with clothespins. Only when you have glued cord almost all the way around should you cut it, 1/2" (1.3 cm) longer than needed. Slit 1/2" (1.3 cm) open on the bottom, and cut out the cord center, as seen in Step 1A illustration. Glue slit end over the beginning end, smoothing edges, as shown in 1B. Glue ribbon around box edge just below lid. Begin in the back, and tuck under raw edge, sealing it with glue. Glue or stitch tassel, centered, onto the inner box lid edge.

2 *Small Box Buttons:* Refer to the photo to glue oval buttons to top in an X, and add a round button at center. Glue 4 flat buttons to each side and to top.

3 *Large Box Buttons:* Arrange and glue buttons in a snowflake pattern on center top. Layer smaller buttons on top as desired. Cluster and glue 3 buttons in each corner. Refer to the photo to arrange and glue buttons on box sides.

140

COVERED CONTAINERS

Dig out those empty containers you've stashed away. use attractive christmas fabrics along with a few trims and voilà— they're recycled into wonderful gift boxes!

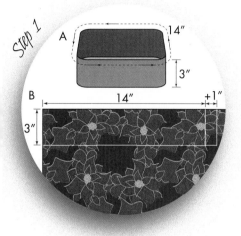

Step 1

Materials

FOR EACH TIN

- Empty oatmeal box, flavored coffee tin, or container with snap-on lid and straight sides
- Double-faced adhesive backing, and fabric (see Steps 1 and 2 for measurements)
- 1/2" (1.3 cm) gimp braid or pleated ribbon, your choice, twice circumference of container
- Trims: mini Christmas picks, small birds, narrow ribbon
- Miscellaneous items: tape measure, scissors, white craft glue, craft fleece to cover lid (optional)

1. *Container:* See the Step 1A illustration to remove lid and measure height from just below top to base. Measure circumference and add 1" (2.5 cm). Draw dimensions on fabric, as shown in the 1B illustration. Peel paper backing and adhere adhesive to fabric, and cut out. Adhere fabric to container, overlapping ends at center back.

2. *Lid:* Trace onto paper backing of adhesive; cut out, adding 1/4" (6 mm) allowance. If lid has a deep center depression, cut and glue fleece to fit center. Peel paper backing and adhere to fabric. Cut out, peel backing and center fabric on lid. Clip curves along edge and adhere fabric to edge of lid.

3. *Finishing:* Glue braid or ribbon around lid edge and container base, beginning and ending at center back. Refer to the photo to decorate lid with mini picks, bird and ribbon.

141

Primitive Pines
tree skirt

HERE'S A QUICK AND EASY PROJECT to BRING THE GREAT outdoors inside. stencil evergreen trees on a canvas tree skirt, spangle the sky overhead, and fuse a whole forest of prints and plaids pines.

Materials

- 45" (115 cm) purchased natural canvas tree skirt with plaid binding, or 1¼ yd. (1.15 m) 45" (115 cm) canvas fabric and 5½ yd. (5.05 m) plaid double-fold bias tape

- Stencils: moon/stars and large and small pine tree or starry tree stencil shown

- Stencil adhesive spray

- Stencil paint cremes: green, goldenrod, yellow ochre, brown

- 4 stencil brushes

- ½ yd. (0.5 m) paper-backed iron-on adhesive

- 8" x 12" (20.5 x 30.5 cm) each 4 assorted coordinating cotton print fabrics

- Miscellaneous items: string, chalk pencil, tape measure, scissors, paper towels, pencil, iron

1. *Cutting Skirt:* Skip to Step 3 if you are using a purchased tree skirt. Fold canvas fabric in half lengthwise, then crosswise. Tie 1 end of string to chalk pencil; knot string 22½" (57.2 cm) from chalk. Place knot at folded corner of fabric, and chalk pencil at cut edge of fabric. See the Step 1 illustration to hold the knot firmly and, keeping string taut, draw an arc. Repeat to knot string 2" (5 cm) from chalk and draw a small arc in the upper right corner for center opening.

Single fold

2"

22½"

Double folds

2. *Binding Edges:* Cut fabric along both arcs, large arc first. Open circle; fold in half. Cut along foldline from 1 edge to center, to make back opening, as shown in the Step 2 illustration. Pin bias tape to tree skirt, right sides together and raw edges matching. Begin and end along the back opening, completely encasing all raw edges. Stitch along the first foldline of the bias tape. Clip seams around curves; trim corners. Press bias tape to wrong side of skirt; pin, mitering tape at corners, and stitch.

Fold

Center opening

Back opening

3. *Stencil Preparation:* Remove the protective skin from paint cremes with a paper towel. Use a new stencil brush for each color. Fill the brush with color, then wipe excess on a paper towel. Begin painting on the stencil itself, then work into the open areas. Apply color in a circular motion holding the brush perpendicular to the stencil. Occasionally wipe the stencil with a paper towel to remove paint buildup.

4. *Stenciling:* Follow the manufacturer's instructions to apply stencil adhesive to the back of the tree stencil. Place the stencil 1½" (3.8 cm) from the skirt back opening with the bottom of the trunk 5½" (14 cm) from the outer edge, as shown in the Step 4 illustration. Stencil as follows: the tree branches with green, the trunks with brown, the upper part of the moon and some of the stars with yellow ochre, and the lower part of the moon and the remaining stars with goldenrod. Let dry. Repeat to stencil 8 or 9 sets of trees around the entire skirt, with 10½" (26.8 cm) between. Refer to the manufacturer's instructions to clean the stencil.

10½"

5½"

1½"

5. *Tree Appliqués:* Follow the manufacturer's instructions to fuse iron-on adhesive to the wrong side of the print fabrics. Use a pencil to trace around the stencil openings, making 11 large and 17 small trees on the paper side of the fused fabrics, leaving ¼" (6 mm) between each tree. Cut out the tree appliqués, then remove the paper backings.

6. *Fusing & Finishing:* Refer to the photo to randomly fuse the large trees between the stenciled trees. Allow space below each tree for a stenciled trunk. See the Step 6 illustration to fuse the small trees to the skirt. Use the stencil and brown paint to add trunks below the fabric trees. Let dry 24 hours before using the tree skirt and 10 days before washing it.

Snow snack pillow

This cross-stitch snowman commemorates the thrilling experience of bravely facing a wintry sky and feeling a frosty drop of Lace Land and melt on the tongue.

Materials

- 10" x 14" (25.5 x 35.5 cm) 28-count khaki evenweave fabric
- 1 skein each 6-strand embroidery floss in colors listed in Color Key
- 45" (115 cm) royal blue cotton velveteen or other suitable backing fabric, 1/2 yd. (0.5 m)
- 1 1/4 yd. (1.15 m) cording, 1/4" (6 mm) wide
- No. 24 tapestry needle
- Polyester fiberfill
- Miscellaneous items: scissors, terry-cloth towel, press cloth, iron, ruler, straight pins, sewing machine with zipper foot, matching sewing thread

1 *Stitching:* Refer to the Cross-Stitch General Instructions and Stitches on page 162 and the Stitch Chart to cross-stitch the design over 2 threads of evenweave fabric using 3 strands of floss. Each square on the Chart represents 2 squares of fabric. Symbols correspond to the colors in the Color Key. Follow the Step 6 instructions on page 162 to launder, if necessary, and press.

144

2 *Backing & Piping:* Cut 10" x 14" (25.5 x 35.5 cm) of backing fabric. From the remaining fabric, cut 1½" (3.8 cm) bias strips; stitch the ends together to make a 44" (112 cm) strip. Fold the wrong side of the strip over the cording with the raw edges even. Using a zipper foot, stitch close to the cord to make the piping.

3 *Pillow Assembly:* Stitch the piping to the right side of the stitched pillow front, raw edges even and right sides together; ease around the corners. Trim the piping ends to overlap ½" (1.3 cm). Stitch the strip ends together to fit, fold over the abutting ends of the cording, and stitch. With right sides together and raw edges even, sew the front to the backing in a ½" (1.3 cm) seam, leaving an opening for turning. Turn, stuff with fiberfill, and slipstitch the opening closed.

Snow Snack Pillow
Color Key

SYMBOL	DMC #	COLOR
∘		White
6	304	Med. Christmas Red
■	310	Black
P	318	Lt. Steel Grey
/	321	Christmas Red
◊	413	Dk. Pewter Grey
4	415	Pearl Grey
8	666	Bright Christmas Red
\	720	Dk. Orange Spice
o	721	Med. Orange Spice
∧	725	Topaz
X	726	Lt. Topaz
☆	727	Vy. Lt. Topaz
♦	762	Vy. Lt. Pearl Grey
E	797	Royal Blue
9	798	Dk. Delft
÷	799	Med. Delft
▼	910	Dk. Emerald Green
□	911	Med. Emerald Green
2	912	Lt. Emerald Green
←	3705	Dk. Melon
▽	3706	Med. Melon
●	3799	Vy. Dk. Pewter Grey

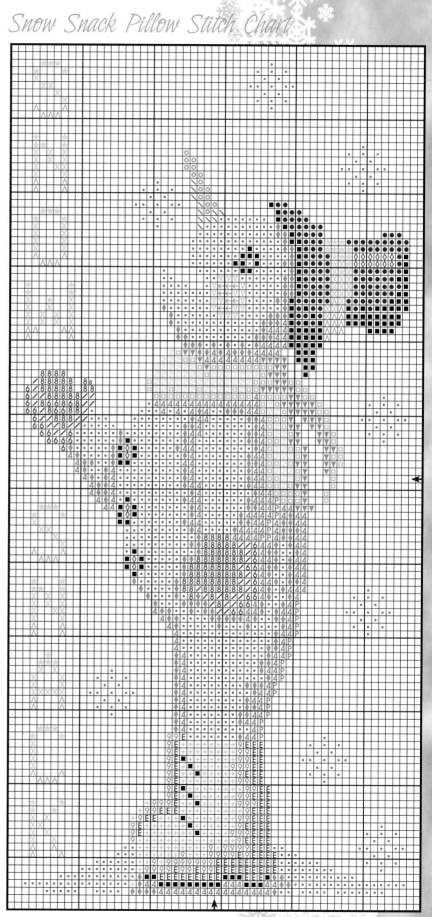

snazzy Sneakers

Materials

- White canvas sneakers
- Acrylic fabric paints: opal, green, red
- Fabric glue
- No. 4 flat fabric paintbrush
- Black fine-line permanent-ink fabric marker
- Fourteen 10 x 9 mm ruby heart-shaped rhinestones
- Sixteen 11 mm emerald green round rhinestones
- 3 yd. (2.75 m) 1" (2.5 cm) red lamé ribbon
- Pattern Page 166
- Miscellaneous items: scissors, transparent tape, colored chalk pencil, tracing paper, old hand towels or paper towels

1 *Patterns:* Use the permanent marker to trace the patterns onto tracing paper. Turn the paper over and draw over the lines with the chalk pencil. Place tracing, ink side up, on a shoe. Rub over the inked lines, transferring chalk to the canvas. Remove tracing and repeat to randomly transfer 7 wreaths and 8 candy canes to each shoe.

2 *Painting:* Stuff each shoe with towels until firm. Trace around all wreaths and candy canes on the shoes with the fabric marker, as shown in the Step 2 illustration. Paint candy cane stripes red. Let dry. Paint wreaths green and cover candy canes with opal.

3 *Decorating:* Use fabric glue to glue red rhinestones to the wreaths and the green rhinestones to the cross sections of the candy canes. Cut ribbon in half; use clear tape to wrap ends tightly to form a shoelace. Lace shoes and tie ribbon into a bow. Trim, leaving a 6" (15 cm) end. Apply fabric glue to taped ends.

turn inexpensive white sneakers into works of christmas art with fabric paint and rhinestones. wear these holiday sneakers to add a touch of glitz to casual holiday outfits as you step out in style.

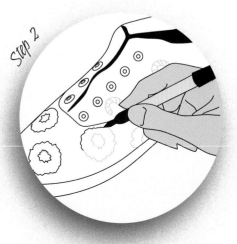
Step 2

Poinsettia pin

CROSS-STITCH THIS classy poinsettia pin to add a holiday touch to sweaters or suits; or present it to a special friend during this season of giving.

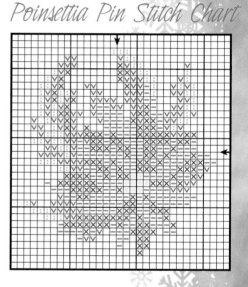

Materials

- 4" (10 cm) square 14-count white Aida cloth
- 1 skein each 6-strand embroidery floss in colors listed in Color Key
- No. 24 tapestry needle
- ½ yd. (0.5 m) black satin cord, ⅛" (3 mm) wide

- Polyester batting
- 1¼" (3.2 cm) pin back
- Miscellaneous items: scissors, sewing thread, sewing needle, two 2" (5 cm) circles medium-weight cardboard, fabric glue

Poinsettia Pin
Color Key

SYMBOL	COLOR
∘	Yellow
×	Christmas Red
−	Dk. Coral
v	Dk. Green
∶	Med. Green

 1 *Stitching:* Refer to the Cross-Stitch Instructions on page 162 and the Stitch Chart. Each square on the Chart represents 1 square of Aida cloth. Symbols correspond to the colors on the Color Key. Cross-stitch the design using 2 strands of floss. Trim the stitched work to form a 3" (7.5 cm) circle. Zigzag-stitch around the outer edge twice.

2 *Assembly:* Apply a thin line of glue around outer edge of 1 cardboard circle. Place small amount of batting in center of cardboard and cover with stitched piece right side up. Press together. Use needle and thread to lace raw edges back and forth across back of cardboard. Apply glue to entire back surface of stitched work and glue to other cardboard circle. Press with a heavy book and let dry.

 3 *Finishing:* Apply glue around circle outer edge. Work the satin cord into space between cardboard and stitched work. Wrap cord around pin twice, gluing second round on top of first round. Tuck in the end; let dry. Glue pin back on unstitched side of the pin.

Can't see the forest
for the trees

This forest will make a striking centerpiece for a dining table, or on a mantel, or as a tabletop display. Add your own christmas collectibles to the scene, or let the trees stand alone.

Materials

FOR 5 TREES

- 1 square each of fusible interfacing and solid or tone-on-tone green satin or shiny fabrics: 13" (33 cm), 11½" (29.3 cm), 11" (28 cm), 10" (25.5 cm), 9" (23 cm)
- Drawing compass
- Gold trims: 48" (122 cm) sequins-by-the-inch; 30" (76 cm) cord, ¹⁄₁₆" (1.5 mm) wide

- Gold beads/sequins: eleven 6 mm stars, fifteen 6 mm sequins, five 10 mm sequin stars, 50+ seed beads
- Miscellaneous items: iron, ruler, pencil, scissors, straight pins, sewing machine and matching threads, seam sealer

1 *Preparation:* Fuse the fabric squares to interfacing following manufacturer's instructions. See the Step 1 illustration to use the pencil and ruler to draw a diagonal line from 1 corner to the other on the interfacing of the 13" (33 cm) square. Draw another diagonal line, 1" (2.5 cm) away as shown, to make the base bias strip.

2 *Tree Pattern:* Draw a line ½" (1.3 cm) in from 1 edge for the gluing lip. See the Step 1 illustration to use the compass to draw a quarter circle with an 8¾" (22.4 cm) radius, beginning the quarter circle along the gluing lip edge. Repeat Step 1 to draw bias strips, gluing lips and 7½" (19.3 cm), 7" (18 cm), 6" (15 cm) and 5" (12.5 cm) quarter circles on the remaining 4 fabric squares, largest to smallest.

3 *Cutting:* Cut along the compass-drawn lines and the 2 diagonal lines on each square to make 5 quarter circles and 5 bias strips. See the Step 3 illustration to cut a small triangle at the inner corner gluing lip of the quarter circle. This will make the tip of the tree cone fit better.

4 *Bias Strips:* Place the bias strip along the bottom edge, right sides together and raw edges matching. Pin, and stitch a ¼" (6 mm) seam. Fold and lightly press the bias strip to the wrong side of the cone. Stitch in the ditch along the seamline to secure the bias strip. Apply seam sealer to the raw edges.

5 *Tree Assembly:* Apply glue to the gluing lip, and glue the quarter circle into a cone shape, as seen in the Step 5 illustration. Let dry.

6 *Decorating:* Use fabric glue to apply the trims, beads and sequins as shown in the photo. For the largest and second-to-the-smallest trees, begin with the sequins-by-the-inch and ¹⁄₁₆" (1.5 mm) cord respectively at the bottom. Glue the trim to the bottom inside of the tree to hide the end, and then bring it to the outside. Wrap around in spirals to the top of the tree, gluing as you go. On the other 3 trees, randomly glue seed beads, stars and sequins.

7 *Stars:* Glue sequin stars, placing the bottom point on the fabric cone top. Glue a gold seed bead in the center of each sequin star.

149

Birds, bells & berries
ornaments

these ornaments
ring out your Love
for nature!

1 Bell Ornaments:
Thread rattail cord through bell hanger and knot. Hot-glue knot to top of bell. Tie a 6-loop ribbon bow and hot-glue to top of bell. Hot-glue holly pick and bird on top of bow, as seen in the Step 1 illustration. Refer to the photo to hot-glue mini cedar cones, mini pine, package, rose, and bell around berries.

2 Grapevine Ornament:
Knot ends of rattail cord and hot-glue to center top of heart. Tie a 6-loop ribbon bow and hot-glue to top front of heart. Cluster and hot-glue berries and cedar cones on top of bow. Hot-glue mini pine, bell, rose, and package around cone cluster. Refer to the photo to hot-glue bird in nest and nest in grapevine heart.

3 Crate Lid Ornament:
Hot-glue craft ribbon around edge of lid; trim. For hanger, knot ends of rattail and hot-glue to top back of lid. Tie a 4-loop bow with bell and hot-glue to top edge of lid. Hot-glue holly pick to inside of crate lid with bird at top. Hot-glue mini pine, cones, rose, and package around berries.

Materials

FOR EACH ORNAMENT

- 2″ to 3″ (5 to 7.5 cm) gold bell; 3″ (7.5 cm) wood crate lid; or 4″ (10 cm) grapevine heart
- 2″ (5 cm) bird
- 1¾″ (4.5 cm) bird nest for grapevine ornament only
- Greenery: mini holly pick with berries, preserved mini pine spray, mini cedar cones
- Trims: 6″ (15 cm) red rattail cord; 1 yd. (0.95 m) Christmas craft ribbon, ½″ (1.3 cm) wide; 1 each ½″ (1.3 cm) gold: jingle bell; mini package; ribbon rose
- Miscellaneous items: scissors, wire cutters, floral wire, hot glue gun

Step 1

acorn cap
nests

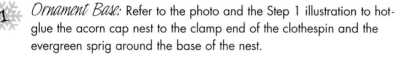

Materials

FOR EACH ORNAMENT
- Large acorn cap
- 3" (7.5 cm) spring clothespin
- 4" (10 cm) artificial evergreen sprig

- ³⁄₄" (2 cm) pinecones, two
- Red or green plaid fabric strip, ⁵⁄₈" x 8" (1.5 x 20.5 cm)
- ³⁄₄" (2 cm) artificial eggs, three; or 2" (5 cm) mushroom bird

- Spanish moss
- Miscellaneous items: scissors, hot glue gun

1 *Ornament Base:* Refer to the photo and the Step 1 illustration to hot-glue the acorn cap nest to the clamp end of the clothespin and the evergreen sprig around the base of the nest.

2 *Bow:* Tie a 2" (5 cm) fabric strip bow. Hot-glue it centered on the evergreen sprig. Hot-glue 2 pinecones in the center of the bow.

3 *Embellishments:* Hot-glue a small amount of moss into the nest. Hot-glue your choice of eggs into the nest or the mushroom bird perched on the nest edge.

Step 1

tiny birds' nests made of acorn caps clip to your christmas tree.

Crazy-quilted dining ensemble

Set an elegant table with these rich table linens reflecting the colors of the season. Gold braid and tassels accent the burgundy and green fabrics.

Materials

FOR 4 PLACEMATS, NAPKINS & TABLE RUNNER

- 45" (115 cm) cotton fabrics: 2 yd. (1.85 m) burgundy poinsettia print, 1 yd. (0.95 m) coordinating solid for placemat backing, 1/2 yd. (0.5 m) each 5 coordinating prints and/or solids,1 yd. (0.95 m) muslin
- 1 1/3 yd. (1.27 m) 48" (122 cm) fusible fleece

- 1/4" (6 mm) gold braid: 7 1/4 yd. (6.65 m) green/gold, 5 yd. (4.6 m) burgundy/gold
- Metallic gold tassels: four 2 1/4" (6 cm), four 3" (7.5 cm), two 3 1/2" (9 cm)
- Gold metallic sewing thread
- Miscellaneous items: tracing paper, pencil, scissors, iron, sewing machine and matching threads, straight pins, sewing needle, 1/2" (1.3 cm) masking tape

Step 1

18"

12"

9"   9"

5"

Placemat pattern

1. *Preparation:* Stitch all fabrics right sides together using a 1/4" (6 mm) seam allowance, unless otherwise indicated. Trim seams and clip curves as necessary. Refer to the Step 1 illustration to cut a pattern from tracing paper. Cut 1 piece each of muslin, fleece and backing fabric for each placemat. Follow manufacturer's instructions to fuse the fleece to the muslin.

2. *Crazy-Quilting:* Cut a 5" (12.5 cm) square of fabric with a poinsettia in the center. Refer to the photo to cut strips and triangles of various lengths and widths from the 5 coordinating print and solid fabrics. Pin the poinsettia square, right side up, in center of fused muslin; baste around edges. Pin a coordinating fabric strip to the square, as shown in the Step 2A illustration. Stitch through all thicknesses. Fold strip over, press seam, trim edges even with the square, pin edges and baste strip to muslin. See 2B and the photo to repeat stitching strips and triangles around square, overlapping at different angles until muslin is completely covered. Fabric should extend beyond muslin edges. Turn muslin right side up, and baste around 1/8" (3 mm) from edge. Trim fabric flush with muslin edge.

Step 2A & 2B

A   5"

B

3. *Placemat Assembly:* Place the placemat backing on the quilted top. Pin, then stitch; leave 4" (10 cm) open at top. Turn; slipstitch opening shut and press. Pin green/gold braid to placemat front 1/4" (6 mm) from outer edge. Machine- or hand-stitch braid along both edges with gold thread. Remove hanging loop from 3" (7.5 cm) tassel and tack to placemat point.

Step 5A & 5B

32"

Table runner pattern

11"   5 1/2"   5"   5 1/2"

A

2"

B

4. *Napkins & Napkin Ties:* Cut four 20" (51 cm) squares of poinsettia fabric. Fold a double 1/4" (6 mm) hem on all edges and topstitch with matching thread. Cut four 18" (46 cm) lengths of burgundy/gold braid for the napkin ties. Slip a 2 1/4" (6 cm) tassel on 1 end, tie ends in a square knot leaving 3" (7.5 cm) ends; knot ends to prevent raveling. Fold napkin as desired and slip tie over 1 end.

5. *Table Runner:* Refer to the Step 5A illustration to cut pattern from tracing paper. Cut 2 pieces from poinsettia fabric and 1 from fusible fleece. Follow the manufacturer's instructions to fuse fleece to wrong side of 1 piece.

6. *Channel-Quilting:* Refer to the Step 5B illustration to use masking tape to mark lines widthwise across fused runner at 2" (5 cm) intervals. Stitch along tape edges with metallic gold thread. Remove tape. Repeat Step 3 to assemble the table runner, and stitch on the burgundy/gold braid and remaining tassels.

153

simply Stenciled evergreens

PROVING ONCE AGAIN that stenciling goes beyond walls and wood, we've showcased evergreens on cotton fabrics. the mini quilt is a great small-space wall hanging, or fill it with a heavyweight lining to make a christmas potholder. use the ornaments to trim a tree or tie them on packages as gift tags.

Materials

FOR BOTH PROJECTS

- Stencil plastic and stencil adhesive spray
- Stencil paint cremes: yellow, green, brown
- Three 3/8" (1 cm) stencil brushes
- Craft fleece: 8½" (21.8 cm) for mini quilt and 6" (15 cm) squares for ornaments
- Pattern Page 169

FOR THE MINI QUILT

- Cotton fabrics: 8" x 8½" (20.5 x 21.8 cm) tan mini dot for quilt top, 8" x 8½" (20.5 x 21.8 cm) black/tan check for backing and 1½" x 35" (3.8 x 89 cm) strip for binding
- Three ½" (1.3 cm) gold star jewels
- Jewelry glue

FOR EACH ORNAMENT

- 6" (15 cm) square each tan and green cotton fabric
- Ivory pearl cotton thread
- Miscellaneous items: tracing paper; permanent-ink marker; cutting surface; craft knife; paper towels; three 5" (12.5 cm) squares cardboard, 1 corrugated; old lace; sewing and quilting needle and matching threads; straight pins; scissors; pinking shears

154

1. *Preparation:* Wash, dry and iron fabrics. Do not use fabric softener. Pin-mark centers along 8½" (21.8 cm) edges of tan fabric. Trace pattern onto stencil plastic with permanent-ink marker. Lay plastic on a cutting surface and cut out tree with craft knife. Save the tree cutout. Mist tree cutout and stencil backs lightly with adhesive spray; reapply adhesive as necessary.

2. *Stenciling:* Use a paper towel to remove film from surface of paint cremes. Place a brush on paint surface and twist gently. Work paint into the bristles by brushing in a circular motion on paper towel. Stencil in a circular motion, starting at the edge and working toward the center of the tree. This gives shading and contour to the tree; let paint dry 48 hours before assembling.

3. *Textured Surfaces:* Peel 1 cardboard square to expose corrugation. Mist it and the other 2 squares lightly with stencil adhesive. Adhere lace to 1 unpeeled square; then mist lace as seen in the Step 3 illustration.

4. *Mini-Quilt Center Tree:* Center the peeled cardboard under the tan fabric and smooth down snugly on adhesive. Place stencil centered on fabric, and use cutout to cover trunk. Stencil tree with green, working from edges to the center. See the Step 4 illustration; tree will become striped as you stencil from the corrugation. Remove cutout and peeled cardboard before stenciling trunk brown.

5. *Left Tree:* Place left side of tan fabric on plain cardboard square. Cover center tree with the cutout; refer to photo to place stencil. Stencil left tree darker along the edges than the center one; stencil trunk brown.

6. *Right Tree & Trunk Shadows:* Repeat Step 5 on the right side of the fabric, using the lace-covered cardboard square. Create trunk shadows by covering each tree with the cutout and stenciling brown paint to the left of each trunk, a shade lighter than trunk.

7. *Assembly:* Sandwich fleece between wrong sides of stenciled top and backing; pin along edges. See the Running Stitch on page 158, Embroidery Stitches, to hand-quilt along trees and trunk outlines. Stitch binding with ¼" (6 mm) seams along top, then trim. Press after each seam. See the Step 7 illustration to repeat for bottom, then sides. Glue stars above tree tops.

8. *Stenciling Ornament:* Place tan fabric onto plain cardboard, and adhere stencil onto the fabric. Stencil tree with yellow. Follow with green, keeping color light at center. Stencil trunk brown.

9. *Ornament Assembly:* Sandwich fleece between wrong sides of green and stenciled fabrics. Hand-stitch together using 1 strand of pearl cotton and a running stitch along tree and trunk outline. Begin at tree top and leave tail at beginning and end of thread to tie a bow. Cut ¼" (6 mm) from stitching line with pinking shears.

155

mr. & mrs. Snowman head

foam balls, beads, homespun fabrics
and straw hats combine to make a cute country
couple for your tree. when you look at their smiling
faces, you can't help but smile yourself.

Materials

- ¼" (6 mm) wooden dowel, 3" (7.5 cm) long
- Acrylic paints: white, red, green, pumpkin
- Paintbrushes: ¼" (6 mm) stencil, No. 8 round
- Two 3" (7.5 cm) Styrofoam® balls
- Fourteen 6 mm black beads
- Cotton homespun fabrics: 4" x 20" (10 x 51 cm) red striped, 4" x 17" (10 x 43 cm) green striped
- 4" (10 cm) straw hats: 1 each man's, woman's
- ½" (1.3 cm) flat buttons: 1 each red, green
- Tan embroidery floss
- Embroidery needle
- Miscellaneous items: hand saw, ruler, pencil sharpener, paper towels, toothpick, white craft glue, scissors

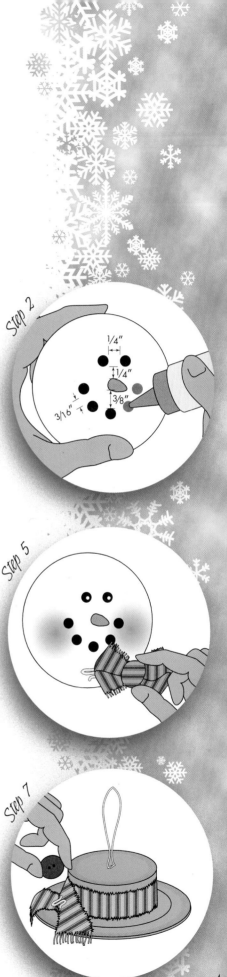
Step 2

Step 5

Step 7

1 *Nose:* Cut the dowel into two 1½" (3.8 cm) pieces. Sharpen 1 end of each piece with the pencil sharpener. Refer to Painting Instructions and Techniques on page 160 and basecoat with pumpkin. Use the No. 8 brush to dry-brush the dowels with red. Push the flat end of the dowel into a foam ball with ¾" (2 cm) sticking out. Remove the nose; squeeze a drop of glue into the hole and reinsert the nose.

2 *Eyes & Mouth:* See the Step 2 illustration to push 2 beads into the foam ball ¼" (6 mm) above the nose and ¼" (6 mm) apart for the eyes. Push 1 bead into the foam ³⁄₈" (1 cm) directly below the nose. Work the 4 remaining beads symmetrically up both sides ³⁄₁₆" (4.5 mm) apart. Remove the eye and mouth beads. Squeeze a drop of glue in each hole and reinsert the beads.

3 *Face Details:* Make a dot of white in the center of each eye with a toothpick for a highlight. Use the stencil brush to rouge the cheeks with red, rubbing the brush in a circular motion across the cheeks.

4 *Hats:* Basecoat with red. Dry-brush the man's hat with green. Let dry. Cut 6 strands of floss into two 11" (28 cm) lengths for the hangers. Thread the floss on a needle and stitch through the center top of each hat. Knot the ends together.

5 *Man's Bow Tie:* Tear a 1½" x 16" (3.8 x 40.5 cm) strip from the green homespun fabric and tie in a bow. Trim and fray ¼" (6 mm) at each short end. Glue the bow tie to the face under the mouth, as seen in the Step 5 illustration.

6 *Woman's Scarf:* Tear a 1½" x 19" (3.8 x 48.5 cm) strip from the red homespun fabric. Wrap it around the head, tying it slightly to the left under her chin. Trim and fray ½" (1.3 cm) at each short end. Glue the scarf to the head.

7 *Finishing:* Tear a ¾" x 11" (2 x 28 cm) strip from each fabric for the hatbands. Wrap and glue the green fabric around the woman's hat, overlapping the ends on the right side. Wrap and glue the red fabric around the man's hat, overlapping the ends on the left side. Fray ½" (1.3 cm) at each end of the hatbands. Refer to the photo and the Step 7 illustration to glue the green button to the woman's hat, and the red button to the man's hat at the overlap. Glue the hats on the heads.

157

techniques

embroidery stitches

BACKSTITCH

Up at 1, down at 2, up at 3, down at 1, stitching back to meet previous stitch.

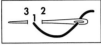

BLANKET STITCH

Up at 1, down at 2, up at 3 with thread below needle; pull through.

BLANKET STITCH CORNER 1

Make a diagonal blanket stitch. Tack stitch at corner, insert needle through loop; pull taut.

BLANKET STITCH CORNER 2

To work corner, use same center hole to work stitches 1, 2, and 3.

COUCHING STITCH

Place thread to be couched across the fabric. Up at 1, down at 2, up at 3 continuing to work tiny stitches over thread at regular intervals.

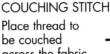

CROSS-STITCH

Stitch from lower left to upper right corner, then cross back.

FRENCH KNOT

Up at 1, wrap thread indicated number of times around needle, down at 1.

LONG/STRAIGHT STITCH

Work stitches for specified length.

OVERCAST STITCH

Use a whipping motion over and along the outer edges.

RUNNING STITCH

Up at odd, down at even numbers for specified length.

SATIN STITCH

Up at 1, down at 2, up at 3, working parallel stitches.

ribbon embroidery stitches

ATTACHING BEADS

Up at 1, slide on bead, down at 2, stitching on according to the pattern.

FRENCH KNOT

Up at 1, wrap ribbon once around needle, down near 1.

JAPANESE RIBBON STITCH

Up at 1, holding ribbon flat against the fabric. Down at 2 in center of ribbon, pulling ribbon down through itself. Tighten slowly; ribbon will curl on each side.

NEEDLE LOCK

To lock ribbon on needle, insert threaded needle ½" (1.3 cm) from end of ribbon. Pull on opposite end to lock.

SATIN STITCH

Up at 1, down at 2, up at 3, working parallel stitches.

STEM STITCH

Up at 1, down at 2, up at 3, keeping thread to left of needle and working slightly slanted stitches along the line of design.

STRAIGHT STITCH

Up at 1, down at 2, keeping ribbon flat. Stitch may be taut or loose depending on desired effect.

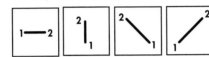

pLastic canvas & perforateD pLastic/paper

GENERAL INSTRUCTIONS

1. Each line on a Plastic Canvas Chart represents one bar of plastic canvas.

2. To cut plastic canvas, count the lines on the stitch chart and cut the canvas accordingly, cutting up to, but not into the bordering bars. Follow the bold outlines where given. Use a craft knife to cut small areas.

3. To stitch, do not knot the yarn, but hold a tail in back and anchor with the first few stitches. To end yarn, weave tail under stitches on back; then cut it. Do not stitch over edge bars.

4. When finished stitching individual pieces, finish edges and join pieces as specified with an overcast stitch.

5. To stitch perforated plastic or paper, count squares, not holes. Each square is surrounded by 4 holes. On the stitch chart, each square represents one 4-hole square wherein a stitch is made.

Plastic Canvas Stitches

BACKSTITCH
Up at 1, down at 2, up at 3, down at 4, stitching back to meet prior stitch.

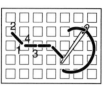

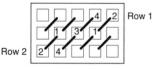

CONTINENTAL STITCH
Work Row 1, up at 1, down at 2, up at 3, down at 4, working toward left. Work Row 2, up at 1, down at 2, working toward right in established sequence.

CROSS-STITCH
Stitch from lower left to upper right corner; then cross back.

MODIFIED LEAF STITCH
Up at odd, down at even numbers, working in numerical sequence.

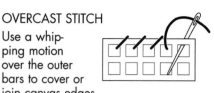

OVERCAST STITCH
Use a whipping motion over the outer bars to cover or join canvas edges.

STRAIGHT/ DIAGONAL STITCH
Stitch over specified number of bars as indicated on graph.

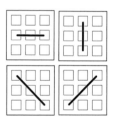

Perforated Plastic/Paper Stitches

BACKSTITCH
Up at 1, down at 2, up at 3, down at 4, stitching back to meet prior stitch.

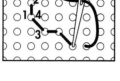

CROSS-STITCH
Work first half of each stitch left to right; complete each stitch right to left.

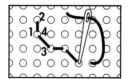

FRENCH KNOT
Up at 1, wrap thread once around needle, down at 1.

GOBELIN STITCH
Up at 1, down at 2, working diagonal stitches in direction indicated on graph.

MOSAIC STITCH
Up at odd, down at even numbers, working three diagonal stitches to form a block.

OVERCAST
Use a whipping motion over outer edges.

painting

GENERAL INSTRUCTIONS

1. Sanding: Many projects are done on wood, and so must be sanded. If painting on a non-wood surface, make sure it is clean and dry. Begin the process with coarse-grit sandpaper, and end with finer grits. A 150-grit sandpaper will put finish smoothness on surfaces, such as preparing for staining or sanding. A 220-grit extra-fine sandpaper is good for smoothing stained or painted wood before varnishing, or between coats. Use a tack cloth—a treated, sticky cheesecloth—to lightly remove sanding dust after each step. Don't rub over the surface or you will leave a sticky residue on the wood. Wood files, sanding blocks and emery boards can be used to sand hard-to-reach places and curves.

2. Transferring: Place pattern on surface or wood, following direction for grainline. For pattern outlines, such as for cutting your own pieces, use a pencil to trace around pattern piece onto wood. Trace lightly, so wood is not indented. To transfer detail lines, you can use pencil, chalk, transfer paper or graphite paper. Ink beads over many waxed transfer papers, so if you plan to use fine-line permanent-ink markers for detail lines, be sure to use graphite or wax-free transfer paper. Transfer as few lines as possible, painting freehand instead. Do not press hard, or surface may be indented. Use eraser to remove pencil

lines, damp cloth on chalk, and paint thinner or soap and water on graphite.

To use pencil or chalk, rub the wrong side of traced pattern. Shake off any loose lead; lay pattern penciled or chalk side down on wood, and retrace pattern with a pencil or stylus.

To use transfer or graphite paper, place paper facedown on wood, then place pattern on top. Lightly trace over pattern lines. Lay a piece of wax paper on top of pattern to be traced. This protects your original traced pattern and also lets you see what you have traced.

3. Brushes: The size should always correspond in size to the area being painted, preferably with the largest brush that will fit the design area. The brush should also reflect the technique being done, which is usually suggested in craft project directions.

4. Extender: Acrylic extender is a medium to add to acrylic paints to increase their open time. Open time refers to the amount of time in which you can mix and blend the paints before they begin to dry. Those familiar with oil paints are most concerned with this, or if you are doing very complex designs with a great deal of shading.

TECHNIQUES

Basecoating:

Applying the first coat of paint to a prepared surface, usually covering the surface and all edges in entirety. Sometimes two coats of paint are recommended. Basecoating is usually done with a flat or sponge brush.

Comma Strokes:

This is a stroke that is in the shape of a comma, with a large head and long, curvy thin tail. They come in all shapes and sizes. Begin painting up at the round head and curve down to the tail. Comma strokes require practice before they look right.

Dots:

Dots can be made by dipping the end of the paintbrush or stylus or even a toothpick in paint and then touching it gently on the painted surface. This technique can create perfect eyes or dots better than any brush tip.

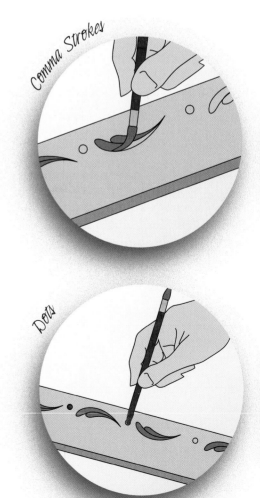

Double Loading:

This is the same as side loading, except two colors are loaded, one on each side of the brush. The colors gradually blend into one another in the middle of the brush.

Dry-Brushing:

This technique is used to achieve a soft or aged look; many times it is used to blush cheeks. Dip dry brush tips in a small amount of paint (undiluted for heavy coverage and diluted for transparent coverage). Wipe on paper towel until almost no paint is left. Then gently brush on the surface.

Highlighting:

Highlighting is the reverse of shading, causing an area to be more prominent. Thus a lighter color, such as white, is often loaded on a flat brush and used for highlighting. Highlighting is also sometimes done with a liner brush, by painting a straight line with a light color over an area to give a dimensional appearance.

Shading:

Shading is done with a color darker than the main color, making an area recede into the background. It is frequently used on edges of designs and done with the side load or floating technique. On an orange background, the brush is loaded with rust, and pulled along the edge, with the paint edge of brush where color is to be darkest.

Side Loading or Floating Color:

Side loading or floating is usually done with a flat or shader brush. Dip or load brush in water; then lightly blot on paper towel to release some moisture. Load or pull one side of the brush through paint. Blend paint on a mixing surface so the color begins to move across the bristles, and is dark on one edge, but light on the other. Make sure to get the paint well blended before actually painting on the surface. Another method is to thin the paint (see below) and mix it well. Load the paint by dipping one corner in and blending well on a mixing surface, as above.

Stippling (or Pouncing):

This is a stenciling technique, and is very similar to dry-brushing, except it gives a more fuzzy or textured look. Stencil, fabric or stippler brushes may be used, or any old scruffy brush. Dip just brush tips in a small amount of paint; then blot on paper towel until brush is almost dry. Apply the paint to the surface by pouncing up and down with the bristle tips until desired coverage is achieved.

Thinning:

Add drops of water and mix until the paint is of an ink-like consistency. Sometimes a specific mix of water and paint is requested.

Wash:

Dilute the paint with five parts water to one part paint (or whatever proportion is requested) and mix well. Load the brush, and blot excess paint on brush onto a paper towel. Fill in the area to be painted, giving transparent coverage. A wash can also be used for shading or highlighting large areas.

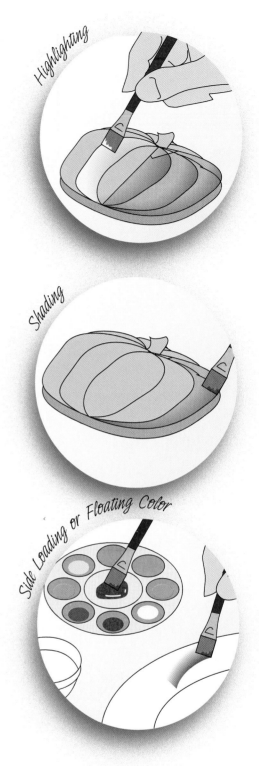

Highlighting

Shading

Side Loading or Floating Color

CROSS-STITCH

GENERAL INSTRUCTIONS

1. Overcast the edges to prevent raveling. Fold the fabric in half vertically and horizontally to find the center, and mark it with a temporary stitch. If desired, place the fabric in an embroidery hoop. Find the center of the design by following arrows on the Chart. Count up and over to the top left stitch or specified point and begin stitching.

2. Each square on a Cross-Stitch Chart represents one square of evenweave fabric, unless otherwise indicated. Symbols correspond to the colors given in the Color Key.

3. Cut floss into 18" (46 cm) lengths. Separate the strands and use the number specified in the project. Stitching tends to twist the floss; allow the needle to hang free from your work to untwist it from time to time.

4. To begin, do not knot the floss, but hold a tail on the back of the work until anchored by the first few stitches. To carry the floss across the back to another area to be stitched, weave the floss under previously worked stitches to new area, but do not carry the floss more than three or four stitches. To end the floss, run it under several stitches on the back, and cut it. Do not use knots.

5. Work all cross-stitches first, then any additional stitches, including backstitches. Work in horizontal rows wherever possible. To make vertical stitches, complete each cross-stitch before moving to the next one.

6. When stitching is completed, wash the fabric in warm sudsy water if needed. Roll it in a terry-cloth towel to remove excess moisture. Press it face-down on another terry-cloth towel to dry.

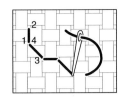

BACKSTITCH

Up at 1, down at 2, up at 3, down at 4, stitching back to meet prior stitch.

CROSS-STITCH

Work first half of each stitch left to right; complete each stitch right to left.

CROCHET

Abbreviations

beg	Beginning
ch	Chain
dc	Double Crochet
lp(s)	Loop(s)
rem	Remaining
rep	Repeat
rnd(s)	Round(s)
sc	Single Crochet
sk	Skip
sl st	Slip Stitch
sp(s)	Space(s)
st(s)	Stitch(es)
tog	Together
yo	Yarn Over
*	Repeat following instructions a given number of times

BEGINNING SLIP KNOT

Begin with a slip knot on hook about 6" (15 cm) from end of yarn. Insert hook through loop; pull to tighten.

CHAIN STITCH (ch)

Yarn over, draw yarn through loop on hook to form new loop.

DOUBLE CROCHET (dc)

1. For first row, yarn over, insert hook into 4th chain from hook. Yarn over; draw through 2 loops on hook.

2. Yarn over, and pull yarn through last 2 loops on hook.

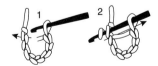

FORMING RING WITH A SLIP STITCH

1. Insert hook in first chain.

2. Yarn over, and pull through all loops on hook.

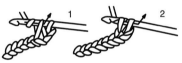

SINGLE CROCHET (sc)

1. For first row, insert hook into second chain from hook, and draw up a loop.

2. Yarn over, and draw through both loops on hook.

SLIP STITCH (sl st)

Insert hook in stitch, and draw up a loop. Yarn over, and draw through both loops on hook.

YARN OVER (yo)

Wrap yarn over hook from back to front and proceed with specific stitch instructions.

Mittens warm
a child's hands

SENTIMENTAL MITTEN PLAQUE
Painting Pattern
Trace 1
1 of 1
See page 116

but Mom warms
a child's heart

CHRISTMAS ORNAMENT QUILT & PILLOW

See page 70

Preparation:
Wash, dry and press all fabrics, including batting. Stitch all pieces right sides together, using 1/4" (6 mm) seams. Press seams toward darker fabric from the wrong side first, then the right side; use steam, rather than pressure.

Patterns:
Trace the 4 patterns onto template plastic with the black marker, and cut out. Label templates and mark grainlines; place on fabric following grainlines, and trace and cut pieces as indicated. It is important to both cut and stitch accurately, so the pieces will fit together properly.

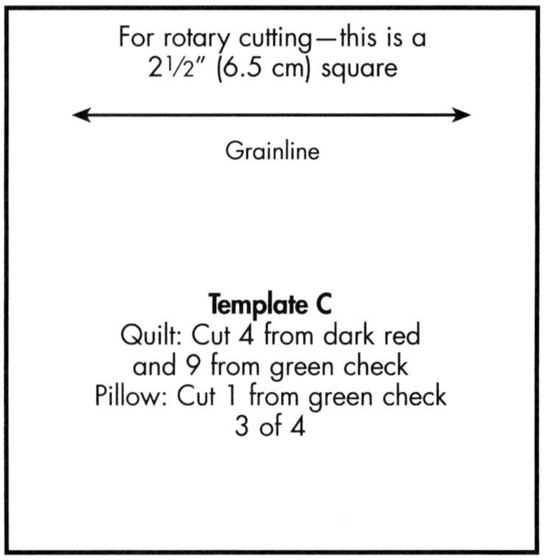

For rotary cutting—this is a 2 1/2" (6.5 cm) square

Grainline

Template C
Quilt: Cut 4 from dark red
and 9 from green check
Pillow: Cut 1 from green check
3 of 4

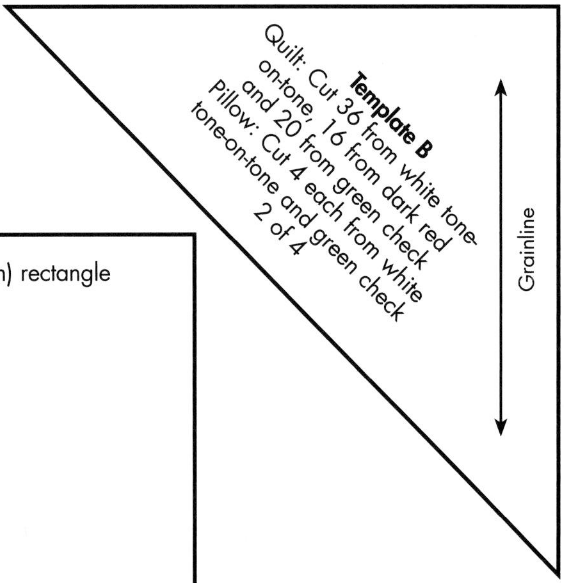

Template B
Quilt: Cut 36 from white tone-on-tone, 16 from dark red and 20 from green check
Pillow: Cut 4 each from white tone-on-tone and green check
2 of 4

Grainline

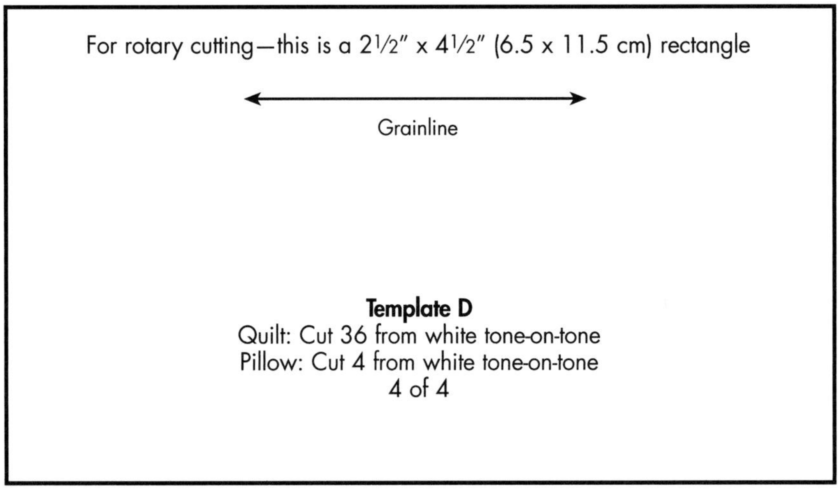

For rotary cutting—this is a 2 1/2" x 4 1/2" (6.5 x 11.5 cm) rectangle

Grainline

Template D
Quilt: Cut 36 from white tone-on-tone
Pillow: Cut 4 from white tone-on-tone
4 of 4

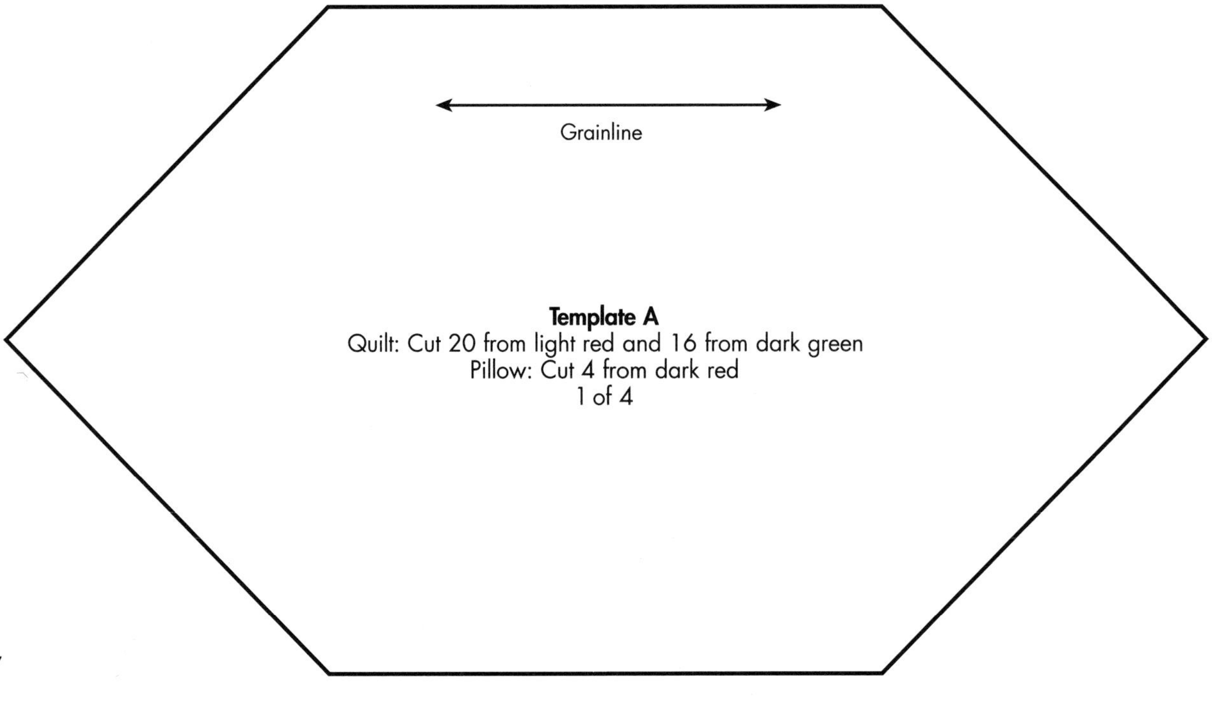

Grainline

Template A
Quilt: Cut 20 from light red and 16 from dark green
Pillow: Cut 4 from dark red
1 of 4

EBONY & IVORY PERSONALIZED ORNAMENT STITCH CHART (3 of 4)

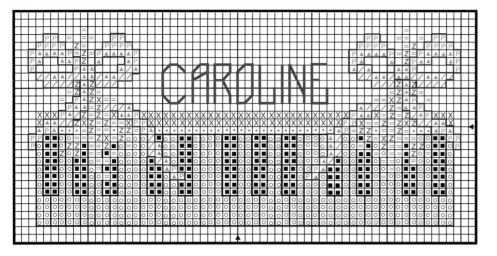

EBONY & IVORY ALPHABET ORNAMENT STITCH CHART (4 of 4)

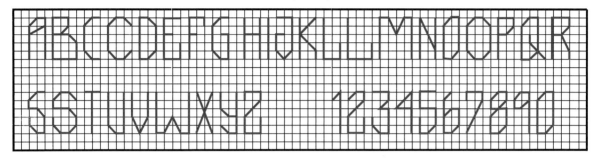

EBONY & IVORY ORNAMENTS COLOR KEY
See page 24

SYMBOL	DMC	COLOR		SYMBOL	DMC	COLOR
○		White		/	3820	Dk. Straw
■	310	Black		▲	3822	Lt. Straw
·	318	Lt. Steel Gray		**BACKSTITCHES**		
X	321	Christmas Red		—	310	Black, Piano Keys
♡	783	Med. Topaz		—	781	Vy. Dk. Topaz, Gold Bows
Z	909	Vy. Dk. Emerald Green		—	909	Vy. Dk. Emerald Green, Lettering
=	911	Med. Emerald Green				
P	3078	Vy. Lt. Golden Yellow				

BUILD ME A SNOWMAN
Face Painting Pattern
Trace 1
1 of 1
See page 104

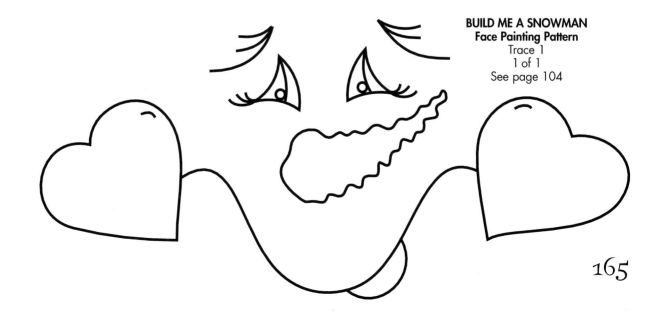

GINGERBREAD TIN TOPPER STITCH CHART

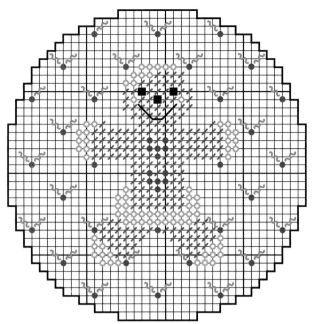

GINGERBREAD TIN TOPPER COLOR KEY
See page 88

SYMBOL	STITCH
●	Red Cross-Stitch
○	Pink Continental Stitch
■	Black Cross-Stitch
╱	Maple Continental Stitch
∿	Holly Green Backstitches

MY TRUE LOVE GAVE TO ME STITCH CHART

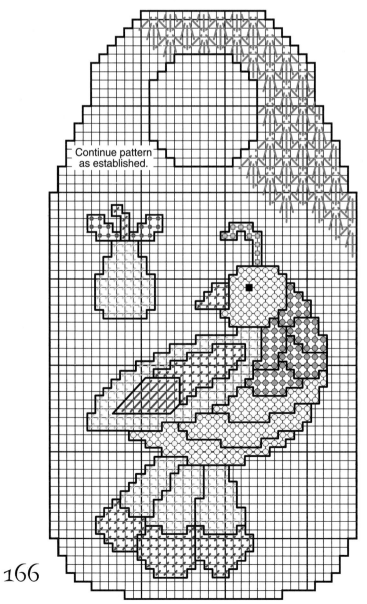

Continue pattern as established.

MY TRUE LOVE GAVE TO ME COLOR KEY
See page 49

SYMBOL	STITCH
ᶿ	Gold Continental Stitch
▢	Gold Cross-Stitch
╱	Copper Continental and Straight Stitches
●	Forest Green Continental Stitch
■	Black Cross-Stitch
◉	Med. Beige Continental Stitch
○	Lt. Beige Continental Stitch
—	Black Backstitches
╱	Teal Leaf Stitch

SNAZZY SNEAKERS
See page 146

Candy Canes
1 of 2

Wreath
2 of 2

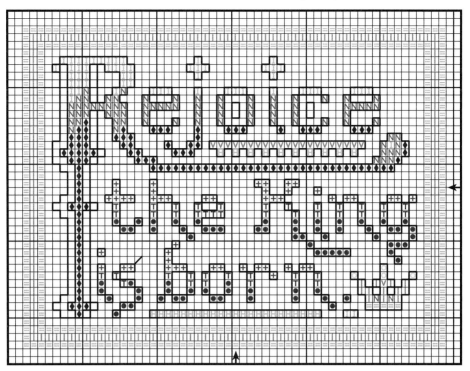

STITCHED SEASONAL SENTIMENTS COLOR KEY
See page 18

SYMBOL	DMC	COLOR	SYMBOL	DMC	COLOR	SYMBOL	DMC	COLOR
■	310	Black	H	700	Bright Christmas Green	●	815	Med. Garnet
+	321	Christmas Red	V	702	Kelly Green	♦	824	Vy. Dk. Blue
T	498	Dk. Christmas Red	≡	729	Med. Old Gold	N	826	Med. Blue
○	676	Lt. Old Gold	S	801	Dk. Coffee Brown	—	310	Backstitches
I	680	Dk. Gold	I	813	Lt. Blue			

STITCHED SEASONAL SENTIMENTS BEAR STITCH CHART (3 of 3)

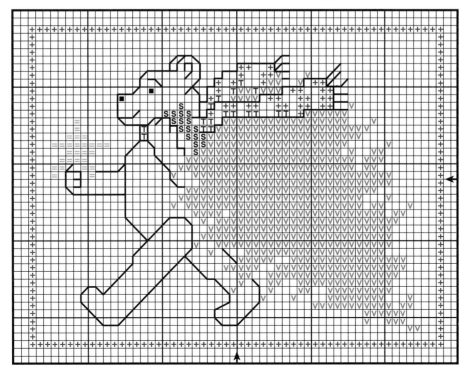

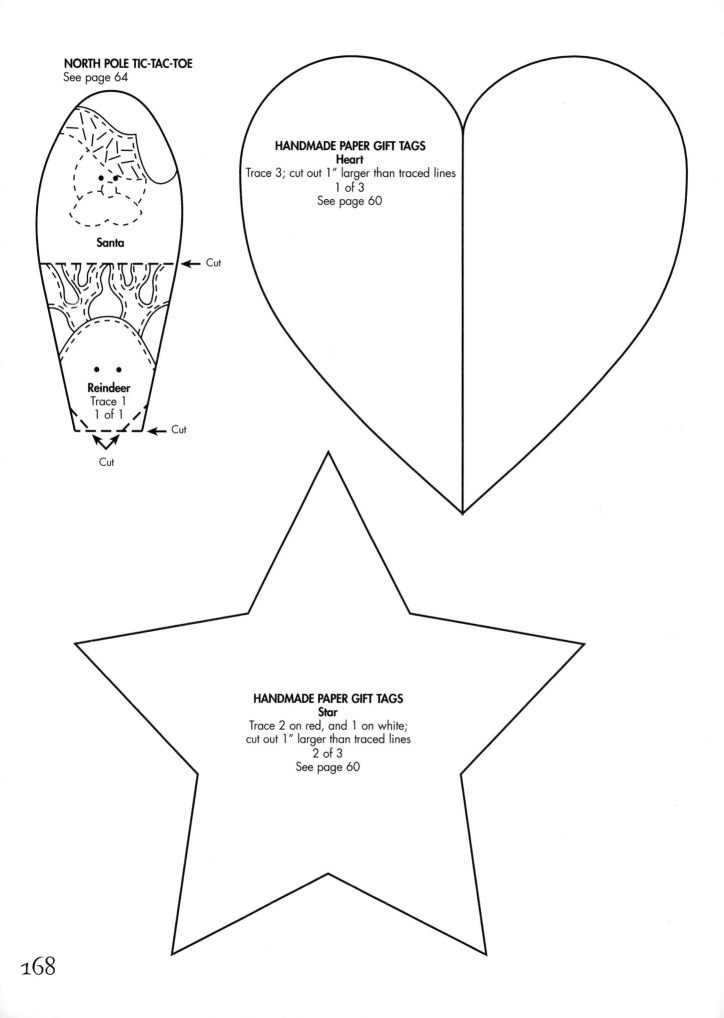

NORTH POLE TIC-TAC-TOE
See page 64

Santa

← Cut

Reindeer
Trace 1
1 of 1

← Cut

Cut

HANDMADE PAPER GIFT TAGS
Heart
Trace 3; cut out 1" larger than traced lines
1 of 3
See page 60

HANDMADE PAPER GIFT TAGS
Star
Trace 2 on red, and 1 on white;
cut out 1" larger than traced lines
2 of 3
See page 60

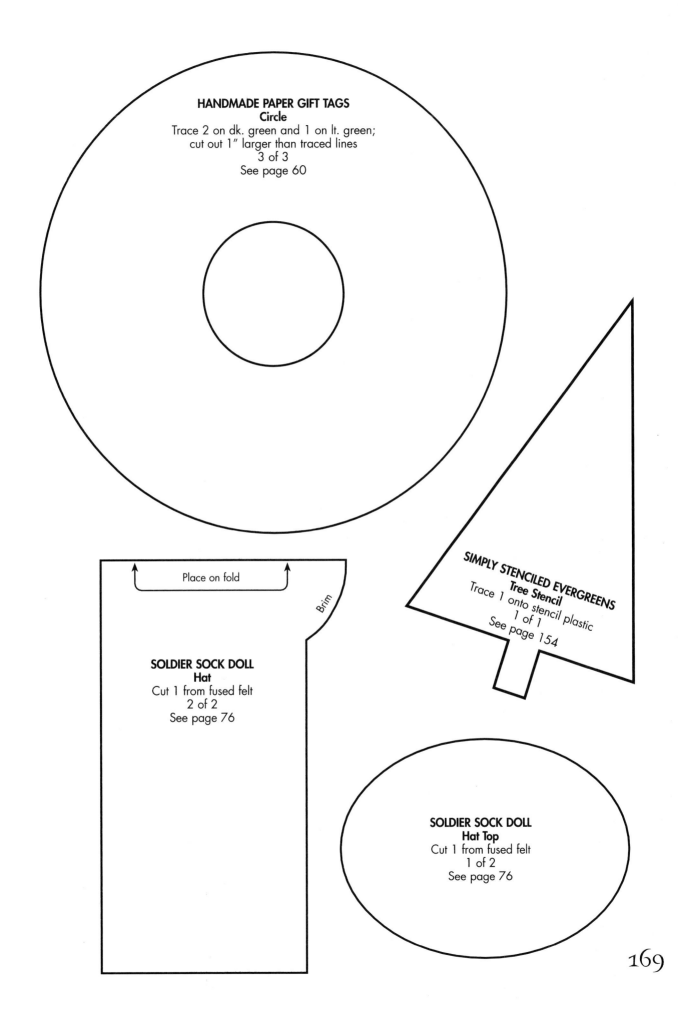

HANDMADE PAPER GIFT TAGS
Circle
Trace 2 on dk. green and 1 on lt. green;
cut out 1" larger than traced lines
3 of 3
See page 60

SIMPLY STENCILED EVERGREENS
Tree Stencil
Trace 1 onto stencil plastic
1 of 1
See page 154

Place on fold

Brim

SOLDIER SOCK DOLL
Hat
Cut 1 from fused felt
2 of 2
See page 76

SOLDIER SOCK DOLL
Hat Top
Cut 1 from fused felt
1 of 2
See page 76

PLEASE NOTE: Inside two rows on each page are repeated.

AND THEY CALLED HIM JESUS COLOR KEY

SYMBOL	KREINIK/ DMC #	COLOR
x	102HL	Hi Lustre Vatican Braid
▲	002HL	Gold Braid
■	012HL	Purple Braid
☼	353	Peach
◇	433	Med. Brown
+	434	Lt. Brown
v	435	Vy. Lt. Brown
‖	436	Tan
∧	437	Lt. Tan
♥	550	Vy. Dk. Violet
ı	327	Dk. Violet
□	552	Med. Violet
=	554	Lt. Violet
\	738	Vy. Lt. Tan
○	739	Ultra Vy. Lt. Tan
/	754	Lt. Peach
✳	3778	Lt. Terra-Cotta
⊥	801	Dk. Coffee Brown
▫	948	Vy. Lt. Peach
—	945	Med. Pink Beige Backstitches

TANNENBAUM TOGS
Glittering Trees Sweatshirt
Trace 1
1 of 1
See page 136

TANNENBAUM TOGS
COLOR KEY

SYMBOL	COLOR
J	Jade Glitter
T	Teal Glitter
S	Sapphire Glitter
G	Bright Gold Glitter
(⊙)	Red Dimensional

172

FELT & RIBBON ORNAMENTS
See page 132

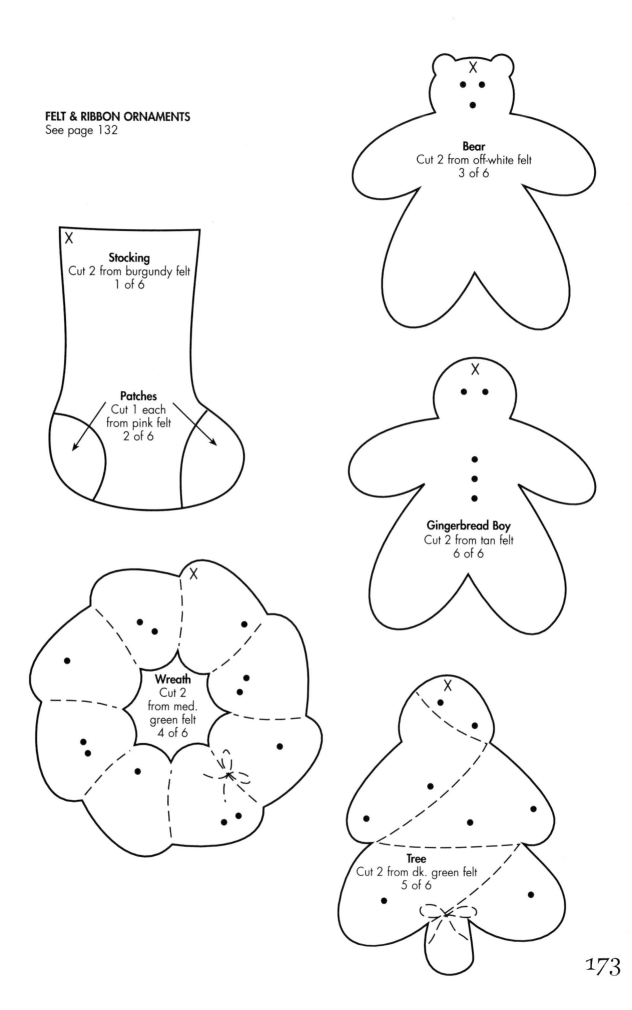

Bear
Cut 2 from off-white felt
3 of 6

Stocking
Cut 2 from burgundy felt
1 of 6

Patches
Cut 1 each
from pink felt
2 of 6

Gingerbread Boy
Cut 2 from tan felt
6 of 6

Wreath
Cut 2
from med.
green felt
4 of 6

Tree
Cut 2 from dk. green felt
5 of 6

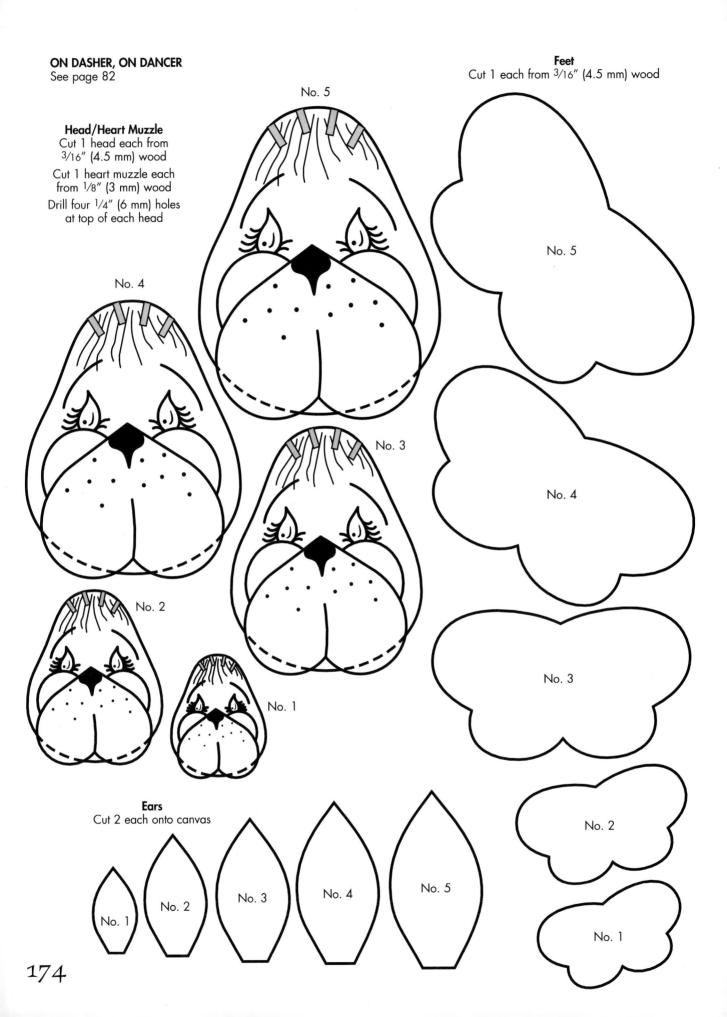

ON DASHER, ON DANCER
See page 82

Feet
Cut 1 each from 3/16" (4.5 mm) wood

Head/Heart Muzzle
Cut 1 head each from
3/16" (4.5 mm) wood
Cut 1 heart muzzle each
from 1/8" (3 mm) wood
Drill four 1/4" (6 mm) holes
at top of each head

No. 5

No. 4

No. 3

No. 2

No. 1

No. 5

No. 4

No. 3

No. 2

No. 1

Ears
Cut 2 each onto canvas

No. 1

No. 2

No. 3

No. 4

No. 5

174

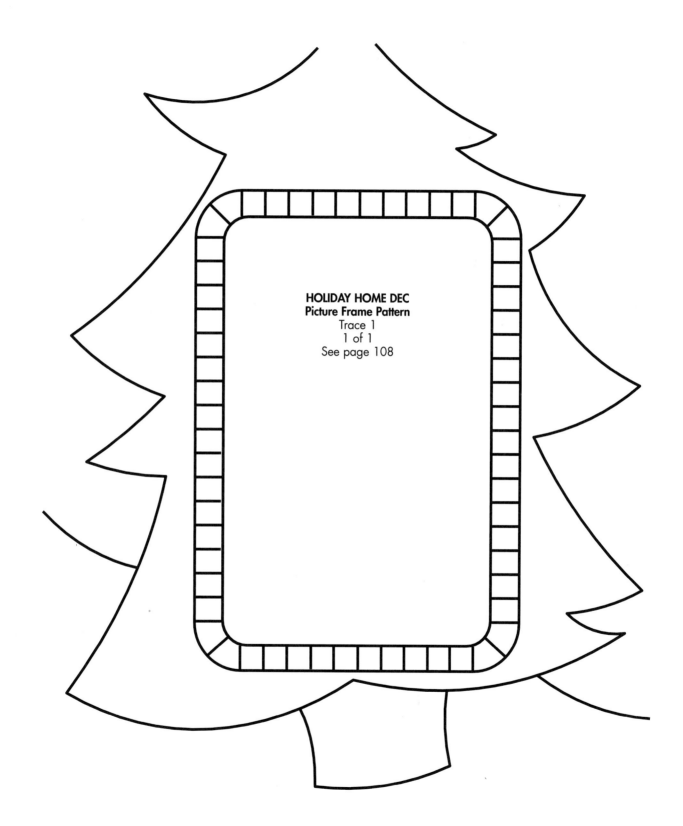

HOLIDAY HOME DEC
Picture Frame Pattern
Trace 1
1 of 1
See page 108

sources

Most of these items are available at your local craft retail stores. If you are having difficulties locating items, or live far from a retail store, please reference the sources listed below.

Page 20, Mesh Star Tree Topper
WireForm™ Sparkle Mesh available from Paragona® Art Products, a division of American Art Clay Co., Inc. Call 800-374-1600 for catalog.

Page 36, Straight from the Heart—Battenberg Heart
Provided by Wimpole Street Creations; their dish towels and Battenberg doily are available from Barrett House, PO Box 540585, N. Salt Lake, UT 84054-0585; 801-299-0700.

Page 38, Glistening Star Stocking
Stocking 4M4471 is available from Adam Originals, 8670 Monticello Lane, Maple Grove, MN 55369; 612-425-7843.

Page 54, Loaded with Gifts
Small Sleigh #12851; 1" (2.5 cm) #4102 and 1½" (3.8 cm) #4103 wood blocks; and Little Wood Deer, Moon and Star pkg. #30020 are available from Walnut Hollow at 800-950-5101; or write 1409 State Road 23, Dodgeville, WI 53533-2112.

Page 116, Sentimental Mitten Plaque
Plaid® Enterprises FolkArt® acrylic paints, crackle medium, varnish and antiquing medium and Faster Plaster!™ Shake & Pour Bottle #67001, and plaster paints are available from Plaid® at 800-842-4197.

Page 126, Winter's Fragrances
Soaps, oils, fragrance oils, soap molds and other ingredients are available from Victorian Essences at PO Box 1220, Arcadia, CA 91077; 888-446-5455; VicEss@aol.com.

contributors

Thanks to the following manufacturers for donating these craft projects for publication purposes.

Page 24, Ebony & Ivory Ornaments
Provided by Wichelt; their Aida cloth was used.

Page 32, Celestial Sweatshirts
Yo-Yo Tree Sweatshirt provided by Kieffer's. Doily Angel Sweatshirt provided by McCall's Creates©, The McCall Pattern Company.

Page 68, Teddy Bear & Stocking Ornaments
Provided by DMC; their embroidery floss was used.

Page 70, Christmas Ornament Quilt & Pillow
Provided by Coats and Clark; their threads, bias tape and piping were used.

Page 72, Stenciled Santa Clock
Provided by Delta; their Ceramcoat® acrylic paints, Stencil Magic® stencils and brushes, Top Coat Spray and Home Decor gel wood stain were used.

Page 78, Woven Pet Collar
Provided by DMC; their embroidery floss was used.

Page 104, Build Me a Snowman
Provided by Duncan; their Aleene's Premium-Coat™ and Essentials™ acrylic paints, Enhancers™ primer and varnish, glue, and 3-D Accents™ design template and paste were used.

Page 108, Holiday Home Dec
Provided by Duncan; their Aleene's Premium-Coat™ and Essentials™ acrylic paints, Enhancers™ primer and varnish were used.

Page 136, Tannenbaum Togs—Glittering Trees Sweatshirt
Provided by Duncan; their Tulip® 3-D Paint™ was used.

Page 147, Poinsettia Pin
Provided by DMC; their embroidery floss was used.